WINGBOW
PRESS

Edited by James Koller, 'Gogisgi' Carroll Arnett,
Steve Nemirow and Peter Blue Cloud

Illustrated by Harry Fonseca

COYOTE'S JOURNAL

WINGBOW ✬ BERKELEY

Unnumbered special issue of *Coyote's Journal*

Wingbow Press books are published and dis-
tributed by Bookpeople, 2929 Fifth Street,
Berkeley, California 94710.

Design by Eileen Callahan
Mechanicals by David Mattingly
Typeset by Robert Sibley

ISBN: 914728-38-5
LCCCN: 82-70807

First Edition / May 1982
Second Printing / January 1985
Third Printing / February 1988
Fourth Printing / January 1991

Contents

INTRODUCTION

WILLIAM STAFFORD
Hearing the Song   1
Oregon Haiku   2

WENDY ROSE
It Was Coyote Made Us Compatible   3
The Poet-Woman as Rattlesnake   5

JOSÉ KNIGHTON
Coyote Is Following the Sun   7

ELIZABETH KEMF
Spirit Song   8

STEVE SANFIELD
A Few for Coyote   10

PAT CARR
Coyote's Wager   12

BOBBY BYRD
Why the Radar Doesn't Work   18

AN'DREA-BESS BAXTER
Coyote's Fear   19

LANCE HENSON
From Cheyenne Country   22
Untitled   23

PHILLIP YELLOWHAWK MINTHORN
In the Texas Night 24

KIRK ROBERTSON
Sunday Service at Short Bear's House 26

WILL STAPLE
When Coyote 28
Raven 29

MARY FULLER
Thirteen Ways of Looking at Coyote 31

PANCHO AGUILA
The Pack 34

JOHN BRANDI
How Many Ways Are There to Tell of Coyote? 37

PETER COYOTE
Muddy Prints on Mohair 43

ROBERT AITKEN
Excerpts from Coyote Rōshi Goroku 47

PETER BLUE CLOUD
Coyote's Discourse on Power,
    Medicine and Would-Be Shamans 49

JOSEPH BRUCHAC
Writing about Coyote 58
Clay 60

BARNEY BUSH
Faces 62
Coyote's Circle 63

GENE ANDERSON
Wisdom Literature as Prayers to Coyote 64

JIM BARNES
Crow I 67

WILLIAM BRIGHT/NETTIE REUBEN
A Karok Tradition: Coyote Lays Down the Law 68

JOHN NOLAND
Origins, Moon and Talking the Coyote Blues 72

WILLIAM SHIPLEY
How Old Man Coyote Married His Daughter   78

MARTIN WILLITS, JR.
Coyote Dances with the Stars   81

DELL HYMES
5-Fold Fanfare for Coyote   82

DON OGDEN
Land Mass   84

PAULA DENHAM
Coyote Boy Is Hungry   86

JOHN GARDNER
Coyote and the Dead Man   89

TIM McNULTY
Coyote at the Movies   97

MAHLON HUBENTHAL
from The Adventures of Don Coyote   99

ROB MOORE
Photos of Eve   103

STEVE NEMIROW
Pissinonem   106

CHARLES GUILFORD
How I Became a Coyote   112

CHIP RAWLINS
Visions   114

LOUIS OLIVER
Grandfather Coyote and the Yellow Dog   116

GARY HOLTHAUS
Horse   119

NORMAN H. RUSSELL
Many Stories   121
The Children of the Beaver   122

CAROL LEE SANCHEZ
from Through the Microscope   123

GARY GACH
Three Poems   125

BRUCE BENNETT
  Coyote in Love   127
  Coyote in Need   128

JOY HARJO
  The Returning   129

JON DAUNT
  He Is Born   131

KAIENWAKTATSIE OKWEHONWERONON
  Ko-ko-ko-io-ti   132

DALE PENDELL
  Summer Coyote Cycle   134

LEROY V. QUINTANA
  Wolf Howl   136
  Carne y Huesos   137

JIM HARTZ
  Shambhala National Anthem   138

JEFF ZUCKER
  Renard and Mooch Watch the Wash   139
  Renard Gives the Politicians Big Mouths   140

PHILIP DAUGHTRY
  The Dragon Singer   142

BRUCE BERGER
  Toyaltita: Homage to Dobie   147

LOWELL JAEGER
  Why Dogs Smell Each Other's Butts   148
  Custer   150

DAVID L. QUINN
  Two Poems   152

'GOGISGI' CARROLL ARNETT
  Answering Service   153
  One Afternoon   154

RUBY HOY
  Grinding Exceedingly Fine   155

Introduction

Coyote refuses to vanish. Even systematic attempts at extermination have only made coyotes more clever at survival. In fact, the coyote's range is spreading—they can now be found in the Eastern (former) woodlands, and in other places where they were previously unknown.

As a myth, also, Coyote continues to grow. Contemporary Indian stories about Coyote keep sprouting up from their old roots. Coyote lives too in modern literature from all corners and sources of the Americas.

We four editors decided to record a portion of this phenomenon. We tried to contact as many writers as possible, by letter and by public announcement in newsletters and magazines.

We asked: Who or What is Coyote anyway? How many ways are there to tell of Coyote—in the broadest sense: the character of Trickster, Helper, Teacher, and Fool? What turns the Coyote mind?

The answers were good and numerous. We worked for months deciding which to use in this collection.

So enjoy it. And keep an eye on your chickens.

—*The Editors*

COYOTE'S JOURNAL

William Stafford
Hearing the Song

My father said, "Listen," and that subtle song
"Coyote" came to me; we heard it together.
The river slid by, its weight
moving like oil. "It comes at night,"
he said; "some people don't like it." "It sounds
dark," I said, "like midnight, rich. . . ."
His hand pressed my shoulder:
"Just listen." That's how I first heard the song.

William Stafford
Oregon Haiku

Coyotes live it up
till morning. They don't even
care what day it is.

Wendy Rose
It Was Coyote
Made Us Compatible

Every night asleep
I am painted by Coyote;
parts of my body
insist on their white,
ivory at war
with red clay
day after day
face and hands
battle
with breast and thigh.

This war is not holy
but goes on
through all the gospels,
all the chants,
all the movements
of healing hands.
I see myself as pinto,
contrast, barbed wire
on crooked posts
across the rolling pastures
dividing deer-eaten ground
barren of grass on one side,

cattle and waist high
African oats on the other.

Why do I go to bed each night
an Indian woman, wake up
white and quiet
as if the woman last night
were someone else
who only taught
this waking-up one
a few songs
to keep her down
and covered
red showing
slightly through?

Wendy Rose
The Poet-Woman as Rattlesnake

[for C. S.]

It was like this today: I was thrown
in an underhand swing to the cibola-city
built of rust and mud on sweathouse ruins.
My people turned their backs, you said.
Cornered, I said. Am I a rattlesnake
that they should wrap their sleep
in horsehair rope, stretch protected
in their desert beds?
My songs are crystallized with venom,
you say, and they must still my tongue
so the life of the songs will become fang-snap,
clamping shut of scaly jaws, a vibration
and a drumming in the dark.

My eyes have truly taken an elliptical slit
and wander in these patches of sunlight,
looking for warm blood to digest;
the radar of my facial pits touches you,
circles you, and strikes, strikes again
til my head contracts and squeezes
the truth from your tongue.

But it's not what I meant by my striking—
if I meant to hurt you
I would not first have rattled.
You pull me out and snap me headless
from my cholla bed; you think
I have swelled you with pain.
You have taken my voice and roped my throat
to a thin wire; you kill my heart,
penetrate it with cactus spines,
swallow it like a roadrunner.

You told me these things
as you stepped in your quiet
up and down my spruce-log ladders.
The long sleep approaches
with its lying coyotes
slipping in my blood
that you have spilled.
A slender joy: that you
lost the war, that
it will take the rest of my life
for my winnings to heal.

José Knighton
Coyote Is Following the Sun

with his basket of shadows,
He unfolds them beneath granite
and follows them into the mountain,
Each shadow is a temple,
but light is the voice
that calls the names
of the green god.
Winds echo thru his darkness
and wear it thin.
They rattle cottonwood leaves
with music like the laughter
children trade for
their parents' darkness.
He builds a white fire
from moonlight that seeps
into the mountain;
then he steals into the fringe towns,
trades it for mothers' milk
while they are sleeping.

Elizabeth Kemf
Spirit Song

Do you hear
The voice from the deep!
*   ajai-jija.*
The voice from the deep!
*   ajai-jija . . .*
—Netsit, Copper Eskimo Man

Some nights

when I am walking alone
I feel you at my heels.
Some dark nights
when I am afraid, your fur
    brushes my calves,
your wet nose nudges the back
    of my knee.
    Oh my Coyote.
    Oh my Coyote.

Your voice has been heard
    even now
and I have shuddered
    at the sound,

the very familiar and unmistakable
sound.
Oh my Coyote.
Oh my Coyote.

Steve Sanfield
A Few for Coyote

Coyote calling
& suddenly it's alright
—this terrible motel.
[*Modesto*]

A LAMENT

Nights used to be
so much quieter
when coyote sang.

Just when you fear
you've heard the last of them
there they are.

The last moon of summer.
A single coyote
               once.
What next?
                    [*the night of
                    Chairman Mao's death*]

SCAT

Each one
always fresher
than the last.

Once again
the call of coyote
—the departing year.

Pat Carr
Coyote's Wager

In the very beginning of the world
the Coyote was more foolish
than he is now. —Yaqui Legend

"He's desired you for a long time."

"Has he?" She hacked at the smoothed stone metate with a pounding rock to roughen the surface.

"Haven't you seen him at the kiva dances watching you when he thought no one was close?"

"Hm-m-m-m." She probably had felt his eyes on her in the liquid movements of the dance without being aware of it.

Coyote leaned against the adobe wall. "That was why he was willing to wager three blankets," he smiled, "and that fine flint knife of his."

"Three blankets?" They had only another blanket in addition to the one she wore, and no flint knives at all.

"Against one night with you."

She glanced up quickly from her work on the metate.

He laughed. "Don't be startled. There's no way he can win. It's a bet for innocents. He can dig all right, with the best of them, but nobody in the pueblo is as swift as I am." He tapped his sleek brown thigh. "These are runner's legs.

The wager is only for the first four rabbits. And then we'll have all the blankets we need, and I'll own that beautiful knife with the turquoise handle."

She looked at him for a second without speaking and then began hammering again on the metate.

He got up and patted her bare shoulder as he went by.

"Don't give it another thought. Badger can never bring back four rabbits before I do."

He went up the ladder.

She glanced up into the night sky jabbed thick with stars like kachina eyes.

She hadn't thought of being with another man besides her husband. Another man's body. Another man's arms and breath.

She realized that the surface of the metate had been pocked with more than enough gouges and she quit pounding.

Footsteps touched the roof and the ladder poles shivered as someone balanced above on the top rung.

She hadn't expected him back so soon. She looked up.

But it was Badger Man instead.

He came easily down the ladder and stepped off, looking long at her.

"You have heard of the wager?"

She nodded.

He knelt down, squatted on his heels to look straight into her face. "I know a rabbit burrow very near the village that houses a dozen rabbits. Coyote was so sure of his swift racing ability that he was willing to bet anything, even something that is most precious to him." His eyes were very dark and they stared unwaveringly into hers. "But the burrow I know of is so close that running counts for nothing. Only digging is important."

She didn't say anything. She'd never seen him that close

before, never noticed how smooth and gleaming his hair was.

"You may tell him if you do not want me to win."

He wore a double strand of turquoise beads around his neck. She'd never seen such rich green turquoise, polished like oiled leaves. "I never interfere with my husband's wagers," she said. Even when he bet and lost her beautiful funeral bowls with the diamond rabbit centers. "I will leave the outcome to the kachinas who rule such things. Perhaps your burrow will be empty when you go at dawn. Perhaps my husband will stumble across a nest of four rabbits outside our door."

He gazed at her with his dark, dark stare. "Perhaps."

Then he stood up and went back up the ladder.

And when Coyote returned, she said nothing of the visit.

But that night she couldn't sleep and stared into the sky hole until the night stars paled to ashes.

In the dawn light, Coyote rose, greased himself for the race, braided his hair so that the wind wouldn't catch in it and slow him.

"Don't worry," he said as he took four prayer sticks from the eaves. "I'll return with the rabbits long before Badger is awake."

When he had gone, she folded the blanket, dressed, and plaited her own black hair with sacred turkey feathers. She didn't know why she felt the need for the turkey feathers, and she said no words of prayer as she twisted them into her braids, but somehow she wanted the eider touch, the quills, against her neck.

And instead of the white corn she'd intended to grind, she took out her small olla of precious sweet corn. She would prepare sweet cakes for the evening meal.

She carried the metate, the mano, and the woven trays

to the roof. In the white blue of the sun she ground the kernels into soft dust, glanced occasionally at the heat shimmers beyond the mesa. She purposely thought of nothing as she worked, and she was on the final grinding when her husband came up to the roof.

Hairs straggled loose from his morning braids, sweat had streaked through the oil on his body.

"It was not a fair contest," he said at last. "But the bow priests have declared that it stands."

She didn't say anything.

"It will be for this one night only." He looked out over the desert that was staining mauve with the sunset. "I will spend the night in the kiva. Badger is gentle. It's only for one night."

She nodded without answering and he went away.

While the clouds empurpled the rim of the mountains, she finished the grinding and carried the fine flour down into the house. She made the sweet corn cakes and baked them in the fire.

Badger came down the ladder without a word.

"I have prepared food," she said.

He nodded, spread the blanket he had brought, and sat down crosslegged as he gazed at her. "The race went as I said."

She served the cakes and sat down on the blanket. It was soft and thick. "Eat."

He took one of the cakes as he watched her. The fire glowed on his turquoise necklaces.

"My husband says you are gentle as he is."

He took the basket of cakes from her hand and put it carefully aside. Then he unfastened the sash of the blanket she wore and pulled her to him.

He was not gentle.

"I have desired you longer than I can remember," he

said above her as he made love fiercely, angrily. "But you were not my wife."

He led her with clenched teeth, led her body into arched shuddering before his, and they lay back spent on the thick blanket. He held her close against his side, entwined his legs with hers as they slept.

Sometime in the night before the stars had faded, he awoke and made fierce love to her again. "I shall have no other wife but you," he said.

She nodded against his shoulder, feeling the knotted tenseness of his arms.

They slept once more, but he kept his arms tight around her.

The sunlight had already spilled through the square in the roof when she opened her eyes. He was watching her.

"Have you regrets?"

She shook her head.

"Then I will go to the bow priests to proclaim our betrothal in the kiva."

She nodded. "Coyote's moccasins will be outside and he will know before he hears the announcement."

He reached for one of the strands of turquoise that he'd tossed aside in the night and put it over her head. He lifted her uncoiled hair to settle the beads around her neck. "Until our marriage," he said.

Then he dressed and went out, pausing to look down at her from the top of the ladder.

They smiled.

After she'd braided her hair once more, she found a pair of Coyote's moccasins, old and stiff, poorly stitched from hide that had once been soaked and had curled in wooden twists back upon itself.

She carried them outside and dropped them down off the roof.

They thudded into the dirt, ugly and poor, the sun's beaten silver eye exposing them unremittingly. She debated about tossing something else down with them, a stone maul, a handful of turkey feathers.

Poor gentle Coyote who didn't know so many things.

She looked briefly at the cracked and hardened leather of the shoes and went back inside.

Bobby Byrd
Why the Radar Doesn't Work

A coyote, a breathing creature
like you and me, leisurely

lopes across the grounds of
the White Sands Missile Range.

Fifty yards behind comes
galloping another breathing

creature, a uniformed MP
(also just like you and me).

At the edge of the desert both
stop to stare at one another.

And the mountains and the earth
reside in the blue sky, too.

An'drea-bess Baxter
Coyote's Fear

This is the story
Afraid to go on.
—Charles Simic

I. GETTIN IT TOLD

I am hungry for all those things I haven't seen.

Everyone worries over poor Coyote.
He's always gettin himself killed.

Eight days and nights with him
and my hair was tangled beyond relief.
Brushing it, he laughed and counted
the strokes in rhymes over and over.

A month ago he vanished.
He's curled up inside a bottle of gin
for the winter.

I'm fighting biting bits of wind
that find their way into my house.
And begin my greatest novel:
Sex and the Single Stone.
(it's an old Indian trick, he said.)

O, he done me wrong for good this time.
Coyote space: how to get the hell out.
It's useless, once he's found you,
you're inside, caught
learning a wearisome lesson
from god's greatest con-man.

II. THE STORY

I thought I felt him around the other night
at the windows.
It was bitter cold, maybe he wanted some warmth.
Come in, I'd say, heat up those bones.
Leave that goddamn bottle outside. Are you
hungry?

This time I'm ready. Coyote always comes back.
He brings a notebook, looks sheepish,
grins Hey.
Hey Yourself, Big Shot.
Been travelin some, aintcha?

Aw, now—he looks so big-eyed and sad
shivering.
But I know better.
I know his pain that opens my heart like a swallow
of grateful water.
O Coyote, master of disguises, runnin and
sweet-talkin
livin off your pretty words.
Getting caught in your own trap,
biting out your heart to slip thru it.

There is more to life than your fear
of falling out of this story.
There is so much more.

Lance Henson
From Cheyenne Country

1
he is rust
        in moonlight

2
when the roadman paused
                we heard our brother's voice

3
one track
        in snow

4
eight without ears
hang upside down from fence posts
near hammon oklahoma

5
the moonlight splashes
in their
eyes

Lance Henson
Untitled

ohkom nivas hatamah
crazy horse and snake on bear butte
make the wind whirl around the prayer ribbons

in the canadian river valley
near calumet oklahoma
i heard the high moan the singular voice
of coyote

so alone
my shepherd would not rise to answer

ohkom maheo shiva domni
warrior heart
moon in the stilled lake of dream

this night i hold my hands out to you

Phillip Yellowhawk Minthorn
In the Texas Night

over the dark flat faces of texas
the moon clutches the night sky like a hungry yellow frog,
the mad heat draws its heart out
and pounds and eats its way west.
a great hunter of bones,
it crawls in the mute eyeholes calling:
I have entered!
I have entered!
already coyote is drunk, he whimpers and staggers.
a belly of fire; this draft of land pushes against his ribs.
he can not close his eyes.
he sings.
he sings.
the blue belly blues. coyote rises
and floats into himself
again and again.

here, the sky stumbles and shakes
below our breathing.
I have sucked in the texas dust and a few night snakes.
coyote, don't think that I don't know you know.
pull your flaming hands away from inside my throat.

I only want to go home, coyote,
I only want to go home.

Kirk Robertson

Sunday Service
at Short Bear's House

he was bundled up
& sent off
to meet his father
the preacher
in the church
only 20 yards
away

he wasn't missed
until
his father
returned
that evening
after services

they searched
everywhere
all that day
& into the next
found nothing
until

Goose Face
found him 4 or 5
miles northeast
of the church
frozen
dead
just a short distance
from Short Bear's
house

I thought
I heard Coyote's
crying
10 o'clock sunday night
Short Bear said

Will Staple
When Coyote

when coyote
is dropped out of an airplane
on a moonless winter night
does he land on his feet?

no.

on his heart.

Will Staple
Raven

I knew her down near sonoma state.
Smell of fields and trees, in a fixed up chicken coop
so the windows were a little low
shy to her assured poise
it got hard to breath near her quiet eyes
    or at least breath harder
the windows were open to cool off
we were sitting on her bed
she had long black hair, black expectant eyes
she was talking quietly
and her voice had a soft musical quality
she was calmly telling me truths about my self
nothing a hand or face or star date would tell her
but with real concern
getting right down to where my blood pounded
my heart to feel my life as I do
calling my shots and telling me who I was
 She looked at me then in a way irresistible
a promise of everything satisfying
    religious and erotic
I looked at her in a trance of lust
my eyes sort of crossed and my mouth crooked
she blew in my face

and puffed out her chest
somewhere I saw feathers
and remembered something like this
"we'll do it your way, I want to do it
like you deep down want to do it"
"you're an enchanted creature?" I asked
for the first time suspecting I was in a dream
"yes, coyote" her head made a birdlike gesture
ducking under her hair like a shoulder of wing
"I'm Raven,"
she smiled confidently
"and I'm going to make you rave."

Mary Fuller

Thirteen Ways of Looking at a Coyote

ONE
Among the neighborhood mailboxes
The only moving thing
Was the ragged female coyote.

TWO
Vision time,
The first glimmering of dawn
When the eye cannot distinguish
Between a ghost and a coyote.

THREE
Her furred, clotted body swung in the wind,
A piece of the night left for the clear morning.

FOUR
Neighbors are not always friends.
This was
Not a love letter.

FIVE
But coyotes are not reliable.
They are tricksters.

SIX

The shadow of the coyote,
Despite cyanide bombs,
Has always
Lain over Sonoma Mountain.

SEVEN

Oh, fat, rancher developers,
Why do you imagine tract cities?
Do you not see how Older Brother
Sings for the land?

EIGHT

I know ancient myths
Of the First People
And I know too
That Coyote is involved
In what I know.

NINE

Even in Death
The coyote
Becomes and remains everything to everyman.

TEN

At the sound of coyotes
Singing in the moon
Even the men of greed
Know astonishment.

ELEVEN

The three year battle is over.
The bulldozers have been stopped.
The coyote is singing again.

TWELVE

The mountain is breathing.
The great transformer is laughing.

THIRTEEN

Trickster turned hate around.
Even in Death
Swinging there in the cold wind
Speaking clearly.
The coyotes are back
On Sonoma Mountain.

Pancho Aguila
The Pack

"Coyote!" . . . "Coyote!" I can hear a voice on the tier call-
ing my sleepy neighbor in Spanish. I imagine him curled
up like a real coyote in his cell—a youngster, with 19 years
to do . . . all in front of him. Another crazy from the angel
dust generation—that clashing iron flower bloomed along-
side the punk-rock garden of hostilities.

"Coyote"—and I think of those money-hungry guides
(their underground name) from the other side (mexico)
who left or died with the thirteen Salvadorians fleeing the
open fiery wound of El Salvador. They came thru the des-
ert like Moses seeking the mystical promiseland where the
great iron princess of liberty rises from the New York sea
mightier than neptune.

But what of the cubans—those hostile angels comman-
deering the swift iron eagles of commerce . . . what illu-
sion did they parachute out of?

—I sense the snicker of the coyote—chameleon trickster
of change—cycling and recycling in the mind.

•

And where does that leave the world? What trick of mind
do we follow . . . what folly do we worship as the path
of sanity?

Peace thru nuclear bomb multiplication? Like mice sitting on colossal death in the breath of life across a long black shadow omnipresent in our consciousness, in frustration enrobing in the astronaut suit wanting to escape in space shuttles, disco acrobatics and the high highest of organic South American or Asian horses galloping thru the veins. The rumbling I can hear under the empire like the rattling generators of cable cars on San Francisco hills . . . reality like Mt. Helen's waits for the unscheduled explosions . . . the tremors coming like the shock waves setting

Coyote and the Red City   田 12 5-78

us down in needle-anxieties of pin-cushions—Ouch!! Our asses are on the line . . . the secular kind!

•

But what of the survivalist . . . the one whose crystal ball is black from inside . . . whose walls hold food, medicine and guns . . . and a masterplan to survive?

He is now coyote . . . looking for a liveable hole . . . vision of a thousand death mushrooms turning to desert the steps of civilization—the very cloak of the atmosphere torn to sizzling sun rays we must hide from in nocturnal existence.

Will we become coyote . . . leading life by episodes of hunts, defense against predators . . . will we live by the moon cursing the sun . . . will our holes become oasis before the plague/rat infestments of millions of city corpses?

(Too horrible these imaginings!) More pleasant the coyote of song and dance—bright daisy smiles . . . make believe fairytales ending in great romance—endless happiness joy.

•

I write my name on the prison walls . . . knowing the ugly side of beauty . . . demon faces . . . moon restlessness.

•

I write my name—like the last man.

•

John Brandi

How Many Ways Are There
to Tell of Coyote?

You need direct experience.
There are books, of course, like J. Frank Dobie's
The Voice of the Coyote, or Hope Ryden's *God's Dog.*
And stories passed on by Native Americans, as well as by
Anglo & Hispanic ranchers, trappers & bounty-hunters.
I've hung around with an oldtimer who's probably trapped
more Coyotes in New Mexico than any other man alive.
Yet his respect for the animal runs par with his trap record.
In fact, he's probably more knowledgeable & respectful
of the animal's tricks, trade & habits, than most
hip Coyote-reverencers who pretend to know the animal
but have never laid eyes on one.
Old man Mack Thibodeaux, he's got plenty of tales
about the Coyotes that've outsmarted him in the past
twenty-five years. And he was the first to let me in on
the fact that the Coyote who seems to be tracking
young cattle for a noontime snack, in reality isn't.
"It's not the meat, it's the calf dung the Coyote's after.
Lickin' good, that hot paddy. Rich with the mother's milk."

•

There are songwriters & poets, Joni Mitchell
& Simon Ortiz, for example, that are quick to point out

that you can know Coyote in a bar, near the edge of town,
in redrock washes, city dumps, jails, churches
or even hear them calling from tumble-down steeple tops.
You can switch Coyote on & off over radio channels.
Coyote calls long-distance from railroad stations
or granite-dome overlooks. There are arroyos, canyons,
valleys, creeks & settlements all over New Mexico
named Coyote. I've spent ten years on & off in one of these
remote places. The locals, especially the *ancianos,*
the very old, have chased after Coyote & been chased by
him in return. They've named rock formations after Coyote
& they've got plenty of stories about Coyote calling
in the phosphorescent nights of August, under the Milky Way.
And there are hundreds of folktales about La Llorona,
the Wailing Woman, who appears at night, changing form,
looking for her lost children, screaming with
laughter, pity, regret, craziness. A teller of La Llorona
stories sticks to his tale & makes no connections between
the screams of Wailing Woman & those of wild beasts.
But I do. A few summers back, I wrapped up for some shut-eye
in my mountain cabin. The full moon was shining brightly.
Shortly before dawn I woke to a series of piercing
screams, each followed by a long, drawn-out gasp.
Somewhere downcanyon a woman was being strangled.

I jumped into my clothes & took off for my neighbor's
farmstead, but halted immediately. The full moon was red,
blood red. It hung limp & dim over the western ridge, hardly
a shadow cast. The screams came again. But clearly
not from my neighbor's. They were high-pitched cries from
my right, up in a series of sandstone clefts.
Next morning, talking & walking with my neighbor, I found
that, indeed, the screams were not hers. And that the
moon had gone dim because of a total eclipse.

As for the cries, I was tempted to pin them to La Llorona
or Coyote, but when we explored the sandstone ledges
we found the impressive tracks of a mountain lion.
"That moon, those wails, my trembling, the unexpectedness
of it all—a true Paleolithic experience," I kidded myself.

•

The Hispanics use the term "Coyote" frequently
in New Mexico. It designates a person who is in between
a halfbreed. A "mixed person, little of both, not quite of
one world or of another." So, the Coyote knows a lot
about either side of his heritage, enough to get by securely
in each world; & to get away with a hell of
a lot in between. I've pondered this usage, & often I've
thought of myself as a kind of Coyote, not quite secure
in the world of humans, more often better off "in the rocks."
I'm content to follow intuitions that connect me with
nature, archetypes, primordial time, & the spirits
that dwell in wild country that keep me on my toes with
a mixture of terror & awe. A Japanese poet,
Takamura Kotaro, wrote most effectively about what
I mean to express:

What is it but the slough of myself that's
    mingling in the human realm? To tell you honestly,
I belong to the family of quadrupeds that live
        on a wild mountain like this.
I'm not what's called a beast
        but a creature totally new.

As a child, I called the Coyote in me
the Dogwolf. This was the "beast" inside me that knew
what regular people thought was wrong, was right.
By following the Dogwolf, I could track through historical
time & re-establish myself with the mythical voice.
The Dogwolf's energy bubbled up from the subconscious

& was fueled by direct experience & quick insight
as opposed to the gaining of knowledge through logical
or empirically verifiable hand-me-downs.
Dogwolf was a totem identification with that part of me
that seemed "right" & couldn't say "no."
A pet name for impulse, the personification
of intuition. This totem still lurks about in my artwork
& seems to be ever-present in my writing.
Some twenty-five years after my ten year-old mind dealt
with Dogwolf, I found myself jotting in a diary:

"Coyote always wants to take man's philosophizing
& turn it upside down. Coyote wants to leap from
the notion of high ideals & bark his passionate
heart out, dismissing hunter & prey, illusion &
fantasy. He can't hold back. He jumps up & down.
A moondog. A true luna-tick. At night he restlessly
prowls. Or nestles down to be swept away by his
incessant dreaming. Poor Coyote leaps out of man's
chest without control. He gives away our emotions,
holding back nothing. No logic. No shame."

•

The Hispanic's definition of Coyote as a person
"not quite of one world nor of another" is applicable
to shamanism, too. The scholar, Mircea Eliade
reported a shaman in British Columbia who spoke
"Coyote language" in his incantations. The shaman of
Siberia & Mongolia perfected the art of flight
& thus was of a singled-out cult, destined to inhabit
neither the over nor under worlds; but to undertake
a life devoted to moving between earth & sky, human &
non-human worlds. The shaman was a Coyote. His "trot"
was bestial, of four legs. It took him from earthly ravines

to those of starry crevasses. Thus, he could understand
the process of dying—in order to help souls
pass from one world to the next.

I am a Coyote, too, when I move between the
male/female, light/dark, yang/yin, within me. Or when I
straddle cultural hemispheres & the whole psychological
sub-strata that accompanies such positioning.
The jumps between, say, green mountain & white desert.
Urban sprawl & Chihuahuan wastes. My isolated base
in New Mexico & the throngs of Asia. The uplifts of America
& the altiplanos of Peru & Bolivia. Immense freedom
but an adjunct aloneness, too—knowing the outward
journey to be only the barest indicator to architecture,
ancient imagery, buried deep inside my own soul.

•

Ultimately, all Coyote tales, all facts from
wildlife experts, all trickster-tellings indigenous to
our continent, do not ring true until one directly
observes Coyote. I used to spend dusk on the
Bosque del Apache game reserve near Truth or Consequences,
watching Coyote meander among willows & sorghum fields
talking to himself, backtracking, circling something
or other with extreme curiosity, occasionally—almost with
definite interval & precise rhythm—turning head & lifting
tail to the four directions, calculating, inspecting,
pondering to "non-think," & finally—breaking onto
a dirt road in a hilarious *trot-hop trot-hop*
hoppity-hop series of antics. Then, for no apparent reason,
making a dead-sharp turn into underbrush;
my vision through the binocs replaced by strata of
snowgeese, sandhill cranes, & musical puffs of songbirds
landing in the marsh, ready to roost.

Old man Coyote—he is omnipresent Creator, the
helpful medicine man, the trickster & the fool. As for
the trickster image—it's for real. I especially
like to pass on a story concerning a laid-back afternoon
a friend of mine spent with some oldtimers
looking out from their back porch into a series of
mesas & gullies, a few rows of corn & a chicken coop in
the foreground. Everybody was talking, sipping
casually on beers, when a Coyote danced up out of a nearby
arroyo, crazily hopping through the corn, each move
bringing him a little closer to the homestead.
This drew silence, amazement & a little bit of laughter
from the onlookers. Coyote was really making a clown
out of himself, being real silly, miming &
stealing closer. But at a certain calculated instant,
when old man Coyote had everyone rocking back
on benches & chairs, he took a sidelong glance out of one
eye & lo—made a lightning streak for the nearest
hen in the chicken coop. And he was off
with it, too, before anyone had
a second thought on what to do!

•

Peter Coyote
Muddy Prints on Mohair

Stand in a puddle of water long enough and even rubber boots will leak. It is not surprising then, that after two centuries of occupation, and despite conscientious efforts to the contrary on the part of most humans, awareness of the essential energies of this continent's plants and animals has begun to exert an effect on transplanted Europeans, Asians, and Africans; insinuating themselves into our psyches and infiltrating our cultures.

Rings, charms, embroidered pillows, cruets, lorgnettes, cookie jars, and clocks with eyes that move, announce the supremacy of Owl as a totem for millions of Americans. Ceramic plates, statuary of varying dimensions, breast pins, drinking mugs, ashtrays and rings honor Frog. Each State has a native flower and bird associated with its sovereignty; sports teams compete under the heraldry of Bluejay, Hawk, Cougar, Bear and Lion. Consciousness of Whale, Baby Seal, pure water, clean air, sanctity of wilderness, snail darter, minute butterflies and salamanders has been the vehicle of massive political organizing. Even the Citizens Band Airwaves are flooded with names of "Tarweed," "Porcupine," "Meadowlark," and "Stink-bug."

Some prostitutes, poets, Zen students and several varieties of libertine have re-discovered the wit and utility of the Coyote-Trickster archetype. They have joined with those Native Americans who continue to recognize the beauty and worth of their ancient traditions, in creating a small but vital host who find value in this half-mental/ half-mammal being.

I count myself among the number whose spinal telephone is being tapped by Coyote. Having spent some time thinking about him, being addressed by his name, raising some Coyote pups, talking to those who know him and his traditions well, and as eager as any to see him gain his recognition in our physical and cultural environment, I am delighted to see hosts of contemporary references to him cropping up in re-discovered myths, journals of ethnopoesy, union organizing literature and Roadrunner cartoons. I cannot help noticing however, the singularity with which most of these references herd Coyote into a limited and already overfull pantheon of American iconoclastic personalities.

Coyote absorbs Chaplin, W. C. Fields, Bogart, Garbo, Dietrich, Mae West, Dillinger, Midler and Cagney as more dated symbols of allegiances to personal codes. His once extensive range of possibilities and adaptation is being reduced to the narrow spectrum of anti-sociability and personal excess. An example is Coyote's (recent) association with Zen eccentrics.

Although Zen training and traditions stress personal experience and understanding (thus the aptness of the lone, homeless, wanderer as a symbol), the three treasures of Buddhism are Buddha, Dharma (the teachings), *and Sangha* (the community of like believers and practitioners). The transmission of Buddhism owes at least as much if not more to those who chose to operate *within* the non-personal, non-eccentric framework of tradition, as it does to those who have remained without. Personal liberation and tight community structure are not mutually exclusive, but in contemporary usage, Coyote is usually invoked as the crazy, enlightened loner whose purity is somehow measured by the number of forms and conventions he abuses. He is never (except in Native traditions) pictured as householder and community man. The rush to overlook this is a Coyote tricking that bears some watching.

I thought that it might serve our burgeoning interest in Coyote to share something of my own experience of his range of habitats, terrains, and markings so that future students not diminish his potential by maladaption, or, make the too frequent error of designating wide varieties of adaptive possibilities within one species as hosts of sub-species. It is to this that I dedicate the following.

Coyote is the miss in your engine.
He steals your concentration in
the Zendo. Mates for life. A good
family man who helps raise the kids.

A good team player, but satisfied
to be alone. He's handsome and
well groomed: teeth, hair, and eyes
shine. He likes prosperity and goes
for it: a tough young banker bearing
down at a high stakes tennis game.

He is total effort. Any good after-
noon nap. Best dancer in the house.
The dealer and the sucker in a
sidewalk Monte game. An acquaintance
that hunts your power. The hooker
whose boyfriend comes out of the

closet while your pants are down.
He's also the boyfriend.

He eats grasshoppers and Cockerspaniels.
Drinks out of Bel-Aire swimming pools,
rainwater basins and cut lead-crystal
tumblers. He brings luck in gambling.
Inspires others to write about him. He
is jealousy.

A diligent mother. Top fashion model
with a fearless laugh. Easily bored.
He forgets what he was knowing.
He pretends to forget. Usually
gets the joke. Rarely follows advice.
Acts out our fantasies for us.

Is in the Bible as Onan's hand.
He's the gnawed squash in your garden.
The critical missing wrench from
your toolbox. He is the one who
returns with a harpooned acorn.

He may be Sirius, the dog star,
who, like Coyote, wanders and dies
awhile then comes back: companion
to Orion, the hunter, who like the
rest of us hunting enduring value and
knowledge, never forgets the brightest
star in our heavens.

Robert Aitken
Excerpts from Coyote Rōshi Goroku

COYOTE AND CHAO-CHOU

Coyote showed a student the following kōan:

Chao-chou was strolling in the garden with his attend-
ant. A rabbit ran across their path. The attendant asked,
"Your Reverence has great goodness and wisdom—why
should the rabbit run away from you?"
Chao-chou said, "Because I like to kill."
Coyote asked, "What was Chao-chou's meaning?"
The student said, "The attendant foolishly attributed a
quality of awareness to the rabbit, so Chao-chou showed
him his mistake by speaking of a quality he himself did not
have."
Coyote pointed his finger at the student and said,
"Bang."

ESSENTIAL NATURE

A student asked, "Can Essential Nature be destroyed?"
Coyote said, "Yes, it can."
The student asked, "How can Essential Nature be de-
stroyed?"
Coyote said, "With an eraser."

THE JEWEL-NET OF INDRA

A student asked, "What is the Jewel-Net of Indra?"

Coyote drew the student toward him, and bumped heads with him.

The student said, "If I had known that, I wouldn't have asked."

LIVING BUDDHAS

Everybody knows how Coyote Rōshi loves to collect Buddhist images. Once a disciple of Rajneesh wrote to him, saying, "You are always looking for wooden Buddhas. You should come to India and meet a living Buddha."

Coyote mentioned this letter to his students, and remarked, "Living Buddhas are all over the place, but a good wooden Buddha is hard to find."

EMPTY

A student said, "I have found that there is no basis for emptiness," and he and Coyote burst into laughter.

Peter Blue Cloud

Coyote's Discourse on Power, Medicine and Would-Be Shamans

(recorded by Peter Blue Cloud)

Good evening, friends. You notice this long, straight branch I'm carrying? It's called a ten-foot pole. It's best used to approach certain subjects which don't like to be approached. Then, if the subject snaps at you to bite your head off, or your heart out, with a bit of luck it'll bite the pole first and you can run away.

You see this old hat I'm wearing? It smells kind of funky, but it keeps the sun out of my eyes and the rain out of my hair. It also holds my head together, which is why I never take it off. By holding my head together, my brains stay intact. And you'll also, I hope, notice the holes in my hat from which my ears protrude? These ears, of course, are my sensors, used to detect sounds which immediately are fed to my brain for diagnostic purposes; for clarification, if you will. You will also note that my mouth is situated slightly below my ears and brain; and the other object of interest, my heart, is even further removed from the others. When functioning, the progression is from ear to mind to heart, then back to mind to be either stored away for later reference, or from mind to mouth to express an opinion of the information received.

Of course this isn't to say that the other parts of the body are not also vital, for they are, each necessary to the other. Like all things within the creation, the loss of one causes an imbalance within the whole.

Take an asshole, for instance, that puckered, smirking thing we coyotes refer to as "the other mouth." The upper mouth takes in nourishment and also spews-out words, often incomprehensible. But the lower one knows enough to do only its job, which is getting rid of waste material, or compost, to put it better.

Speaking of assholes, I knew a young fellow once, about one-tenth as smart as he claimed to be. Lost his asshole one time because he forgot to listen. He was out gathering mushrooms when one of them spoke to him and said, "I am a medicine. Don't pick me!" He immediately plucked the mushroom from the ground and popped it into his mouth: figured, hell, if this is medicine maybe it'll do something wonderful and strange for me. (For of course this young fellow was never happy or healthy, being always too busy telling others how to live to take the time to take care of himself.) Well, he got really sick. Vomited, farted and shit all over himself. Shit so much, in fact, that his asshole fell off without him even knowing. Probably still running around looking for it. Yes, he's the first person I ever met with a detachable asshole.

Anyway, I'm here tonight to speak of medicine and those some call shamans. I need the money you're paying to hear about these subjects. So, okay. I just mentioned both in one sentence and that's probably a beginning.

And now I want to tell you about a young woman I met at a famous university campus. Met her at a party. She walked right up to me and started looking at me through a crystal. She looked and looked, then told me very serious-ly: "I'm a medicine woman, you know; You must come to see me." I kept a very serious look on my own face and told her solemnly, "Yes, I will come to see you. What is your name and address?" "Oh," she said, hesitating momentarily, "Shamaness Fast-Walker. Meet me by that big oak up the hill. Right after the party." Then she walked away to crystal a few others.

She was pretty good-looking, so I went and met her later. Asked her to put her pouch of crystals behind the oak, then we got down to the business of the two-backed dance and other forms of strenuous frivolity. After our final performance, which was a take-off on aerial acrobatics done hanging from an oak branch, she retrieved her crystals and proceeded to "do me," as she called it. It was a full moon night. The stars glittered and danced within the crystal.

I'd learned very young to counteract powers I had not requested. I stared back at her through the crystal. She began fading. I could see the moon through her body. Her eyes dimmed and her mouth opened to plead with me. But it was too late. I couldn't stop myself. She faded completely away, not even leaving the trace of a shadow.

Someday I'll bring her back. She did know some good tricks, though they had more to do with body magic.

I went to another party on the same campus, given to celebrate the arrival of a well-known poet. His fame was based on the fact that he was, quote: "A Shaman Poet!" Now that's really heavy, I thought, settling down with the others to hear his poems. He began chanting his poems in a deep, slow voice. Every other line spoke of his powers to understand all things within the creation. His choruses called on his powers to hear him, to reaffirm these powers.

He was beautiful, his long hair swaying in rhythm to his body movements, his white-streaked beard jutting out in profound wisdom. I was very impressed. I looked around at the others and saw that they were as if in a trance. His words and motions had acted to put everyone under his spell. Oh, he had power all right, real magnetism.

I reached for him with my mind, to share some of that strength. I touched a shell and put my ear to it. I heard the echos of his own words bouncing back and forth within the hollow shell. Then I probed his mind. I went inside of it to find a tight bundle of self, a bursting ball of energy looking out of eyes which were intent only on seducing his audience.

I felt sad. I withdrew and sat with the others. I'd stopped listening, for I was depressed. Here is no shaman, I thought, here is a powerful mind centered on self.

Being a creature native to this continent, I'm often accused of siding with my indigenous relatives. I deny this and will state at this time that power and wisdom are universal. No one center of this earth possesses the allness of power. I would also like to say at this time that phonies, too, are universal. But then perhaps, like decay, the phonies are necessary compost to the growth of real power. But who can know?

Take a drum, and a rattle. Take a people sitting in circle around a fire, singing songs of the creation. The very same songs their ancestors sang.

Now take the same people and let a flea of dissatisfaction bite one of them. A young man (let's pick on him) takes the drum passed to him by an elder. Even before he consents to begin drumming, he must first change the painted designs on the drum. Then he removes the feathers and replaces them with bells. Now he's ready. He begins the ancient beat, then hesitates. It is too slow. Se he speeds up the beat to satisfy and keep pace with his quick mind. The song is new. The people listen respectfully seeking to share a newness. But the young man is still not satisfied, and before the people can begin to comprehend his song, he has begun another. Then quickly he does variations on the theme until the theme itself has been lost, swallowed up in his frenzy. Even he has forgotten the original theme. "Well," he says in explanation, "that's progress."

Sort of reminds me of a pup when it's agitated for some reason and begins chasing and biting at its own tail. That's what's called, "a tight circle of concentration."

Where was I? Seems like I'm going in circles myself, don't it? Do I seem bitter or anything? I hope not, after all I want you to invite me back.

Yes, well, the first time it happened was so long ago that even I barely remember. It was a girl child out walking through the forest alone. But not alone, because the little people were curious and followed her. She was out walking because she felt bad. Her father had been hurt while hunting. He'd cut open his leg on a branch sticking from a tree at ground level. He'd been too eager, he admitted to his family. Game was scarce and he was trying too hard and had forgotten caution. It was his own fault, he insisted. And now the cut was swollen with puss and would not heal.

And so the little girl was walking, trying to keep herself from crying. Tears were not much of a cure for physical pain, she knew. The little people sensed her great sorrow and decided to let her see them. They wanted to know why she was feeling such sorrow.

They let themselves be seen by her. She'd always known they lived in these woods, but this was the first time she'd seen them. They were all very formal as they introduced one another. They liked her very much, and felt a deep respect for her sorrow.

Asking politely the source of her sorrow, after they got to know her, she told them all. The little people sat with her in silence for a long time. Finally, one of them spoke softly, telling the girl to continue her walk, and to pay close attention to everything she passed.

The girl continued on into the forest, watching and listening. In a clearing, as she was stepping across a small brook, she heard a tiny, polite cough. She looked all around, but couldn't find the source. Then the cough was repeated and she looked down. There, right next to her, a small green plant was nodding and moving its leaves. There being no breeze and it being the only thing around in motion, the child knelt to study the plant.

It spoke to her then, apologizing for coughing and interrupting her walk. The plant explained that the little people had asked it to help her. It then told her that it possessed a power of curing. It would teach the girl its powers if she would take the time to learn how to use it properly. The process was involved, but was soon learned by the girl. It involved a cleansing, a chant, a song, a slow process of preparation, a further singing to be shared by the person being cured, and this was to be followed by a thank-you feast for the people of the creation. The plant emphasized that the thank-you not be made to the plant itself, but to all things within the creation.

The child picked the plant and some of its relatives as instructed and returned home. She told her family of the gift she'd been given, and then prepared the cure. Her father was cured so quickly that he was able to go out and hunt the very food which was used for the thank-you feast.

The girl child grew to maturity and became known as a curing person. She always followed the first instructions given by the plant, step by step slowly, so that she made no mistake. As she grew in mind and body, so too grew her knowledge of medicine, for the little people never ceased to talk to her even in her old age. And as time passed, she was given to know many other curing plants, one by one as they were needed.

She shared her knowledge with a few others, so that it would stay alive within her tribe. Not everyone is given the patience to learn the curing arts. Many other skills are needed with a tribe to assure survival. Usually, as a person grows, their own particular skill will manifest itself. As with everything else, when all the arts and skills are combined, a strong unity exists within the tribe.

And within all this I'd like to add that I've never yet met a person of power (except myself) who gives themselves titles such as medicine person, power person, or shaman. Even within a tribe or nation, the people know who to see for their particular needs, so why give them titles?

When porcupine goes night walking, he doesn't look behind himself and say, "Ah, yes, I got my quills with me," he knows what he's got.

And now I'd like to end all this with a little question and answer song I took the liberty of composing once, after being besieged by an audience. It's called, Coyote, Coyote, please tell me, and goes like this:

Coyote, coyote, please tell me,
What is a shaman?

A shaman I don't know
anything about.
I'm a doctor, myself.
When I use medicine,
it's between me,
my patient, and the creation.

Coyote, coyote, please tell me,
What is power?

It is said that power
is the ability to start
your chainsaw
with one pull.

Coyote, coyote, please tell me,
What is magic?

Magic is the first taste
of ripe strawberries, and
magic is a child dancing
in a summer's rain.

Coyote, coyote, please tell me,
Why is creation?

Creation is because I
went to sleep last night
with a full stomach.
And when I woke up
this morning,
everything was here.

Coyote, coyote, please tell me,
Who you belong to?

According to the latest
survey,
there are certain persons,
who,
in poetic or scholarly guise,
have claimed me
like a conqueror's prize.

Let me just say
once and for all
just to be done:
        Coyote
he belongs to none.

Well, my friends, that's about it. As you leave you may
notice a little basket sitting by the door. It's called a hunger
basket, and if you would be good enough to feed it a little
money, it will be a very happy basket.

Thank you.

Joseph Bruchac
Writing About Coyote

Closing my eyes,
I see you, Coyote
with your eyes of a dangerous old man
who'd eat up his own grandchildren
just to give birth to them again.
I hear your laughing voice,
full of stones and raw meat.

You trot, looking back.
Your feet say Follow Me
and I remember the Adirondack forest
just upslope from the Cedar River.
Snow flakes curtained the trees
as I shot at your shadow
zig-zagging among pines
until you came close enough
to touch my boot, then whirled
into the wind, vanished,
gunshot echoes bouncing back,
footprints filling with white
and half of my breath gone with you.

I have held this memory
like a talking stone
till my years were ready,
my hands less eager
to hurl crazy power
and now I have given it
back to you.

Joseph Bruchac
Clay

Old Man said in the dream
you'd pass this way
where the streams have lifted
their long dresses to flow
away all traces of order
a culvert turned sideways
a rock bridge broken
and everything wiped clay-clean,
featureless as the start of spring.

By the bend the big cedar,
webs of insect and arachnid
woven into its cracked bark,
tells you to stop, squat
under its shelter, look down
where the rain dapples water
rippling clear above its bed.

There, at the edge, are
Coyote's footprints and
the signs of digging
as if something were molded
and just beyond,

half wiped away,
a new print which almost
has the shape of a human hand.

Barney Bush

Faces

Across the hollow
dogs bark when there is
only a wind
Two faces caught between
Ohio villages and a time warp
built by calloused European and
Chinese hands   sit late into
night
listening by kerosene lamp
Coyotes   long shrill   edge of
field almost laughing in
competitive cries   knowing
well-fed dogs cannot
follow wild wind
Coyote hears all movement of
every season   even sightseers
          stomachs filled with
cow and hog meat   stalking the wild
they seldom taste hear only the
sound of their guns
Who laughs in this fading light
Two faces of yellow lamp   smile
across to each other behind
coyote eyes.

Barney Bush
Coyote's Circle

Corn drying on Tulsa newspapers
half circling the well
over stories of earthquakes
train wrecks and Russians in Cuba
   no singing
   no drumming
brown suncreased hands work
the earth furrowing graves
seed to lie dormant
after this last harvest

Cousins take me far
mountain's edge to hear
coyote's singing
higher
this edge we sing
like coyote's starry night
   crying my coming
   crying my leaving
World of insane eyes closing in

On Amtrack south
college peoples' eyes   barren earth
closing inside them

latching onto new world salvation
new world brotherhood
new world sisterhood
looking for ways out from
disaster their families
blindly worked for

He was a voice for the
Nationalist People's Party
severe eyes unblurred   his voice
sure
said welcome to Pre-World War Three
riding this train
Only my ears turned to hear
coyote's barking out past the train's
light
out through lowland darkness
out into the edge of America's
cornfields
to lodges where drums and
songs are inside bodies
waiting.

Gene Anderson
Wisdom Literature
as Prayers to Coyote

Walking in grass and wind
I meet meadowlarks,
flocks around me
singing in barley.

My gardens of Paradise
are vast dry fields
of Pigeon Pass
and Moreno Valleys.

My trees are life
are worn olive
and orange trees
in abandoned orchards.

My firmament of Heaven
is bare granite rock
that flakes in desert sun
to stony adobe clay.

Coyote of the sky,
leave my door open.

Leave me
this dusty road.

Make the great field
of hard barley
an endless way
for my feet.

Jim Barnes
Crow I

A crow calls from the ridge. Twice. Three times. I pinch my nose gently, cupping my left hand over the bridge of my nose. I caw the way the sawmillers taught me. I am a fool to think I can fool the crow. I caw. Twice. Three times. I see the black wings settle softly in on limbs high above my head. I never knew it would come to this. How I continue the conversation is exactly the point in question. Like an idiot, I put my hands in my pockets and stretch my arms with senseless glee. The crow preens his feathers, gives me sidewise looks. He drops like lead to eye level. The low limb twangs. I can see the world behind me in his black pupils.

William Bright and Nettie Reuben
A Karok Tradition:
Coyote Lays Down the Law

Kunpiip,
  "Xâatik áppap yúruk uvuunúpahiti,
  káru áppap káruk uvuunôovuti,
    xâatik vaa ukupiti."
Kári xás cémmi,
  vaa uum vúra payúruk tákunvíitrup,
  tuzívruuhrup,
    yúruk.
Izyáruk kúna úpviitroovees,
  uzivruuhroovees káru,
    káruk uvuunôvahiti,
      pa'íssaha.
Kári xás Pihnêefic upiip,
  "Pûuhara!
    Xáyfaat vaa ukupiti,
      koovúra yúruk kámvuunupahiti.
"Vaa uum vúra káan ifmaaráppiit kamíktaatroovuti,
  káruk uvítroovuti."
Kári xás kúna kunpiip,
  "Asiktávaan pamukun'áttiman máruk tákunsánnaan,
  púyava máruk xás áhup sú' tákunmáhyaan,
    túr tákuníkyav.
"Kári xás tákunpávyiihsip pa'asiktávaansa.

People once said,
    "Let the river flow DOWNstream on one side,
        and UPstream on the other side,
            let it be that way."
So all right,
    when they traveled DOWNstream by boat,
        they drifted down,
            downstream.
But they'd travel back up on the other side of the river,
    they'd drift upstream too,
        as it flowed UPstream,
            that water.
And then Coyote said,
    "Not at all!
        Let it not be that way,
            let it all flow DOWNstream.
"Let the young husbands have to push their way up there,
    when they travel UPstream."
And then again people said,
    "Women carry their packbaskets UPhill,
        up there they put wood in them,
            they make basketloads.
"Then the women leave for home.

"Kári xás vaa vúra káan tákun'iitsur,
   pamukúntur."
Xás kunpiip,
   "Vaa vúra kun'írunaatihees,
      pattur."
Kári xás Pihnêefic uppiip,
   "Xáyfaat!
      Pûuhara!
         Vúra uum yararáppiit vúra kámtuunti."
Kári xás vaa ukupíti,
   payêem tápu'áhootihara,
      pattur.

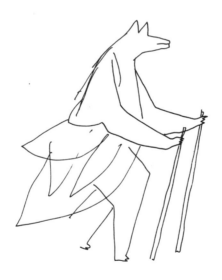

"And they just leave them there,
   those basketloads."
And they said,
   "They'll just WALK home,
      those basketloads."
And then Coyote said,
   "Don't do that!
      Not at all!
         Let the young wives just CARRY the loads."
So that's how it is,
   now they don't walk any more,
      those basketloads."

John Noland
Origins, Moon &
Talking the Coyote Blues

One day when Grandfather Coyote was very young he was wandering through the blue dusk of dreamtime when he came to a ravine in the river breaks that he had never explored. He entered it with the casual grace of the very young who do not know what they do. Soon he came to a large boulder, a white limestone boulder shaped like a woman. Immediately Coyote's starfish fingers itched. He rubbed, and as he rubbed he dreamed.

Now Coyote was still a very young man and naturally his dreams were of a very young woman—coyote-woman. He rubbed the long plains of her limestone belly, he rubbed the juttings of her outcropped breasts, his fingers twinkled along the ridge of her back, then slowly, starfish-like, they crept toward a darkened crevice that whispered the green and pungent cry of sea. As he dreamed and rubbed, though he did not notice, the stone beneath his hand lit with the tiny glow of a fire opal.

"Come Coyote, enter my door," a voice called.

It sounded to him like the voice of the Great and Monstrous Catfish, but it was greener, lighter. It whispered with the laughter of sunflowers and bluebells. And where it whispered Coyote saw a cave. He entered and was caught in a swirl of passages winding deeper and deeper into the earth. Below him he could hear the swish and suck of inland waves as they ebbed and flowed among the distant boulders.

He emerged into a small room lit with leaf-green light. In the center was a pool. A cup rested beside the pool and a voice said, "After your journey you must be thirsty, Coyote. Here, drink some of this."

The voice whispered through Coyote's ears, siren-like, and the deep song of the land and the flesh rose up, calling him towards the pool.

Coyote grinned and lifted the cup. He glanced quickly around looking for the voice, but he saw no one. Swaggering, he drank the liquid from the cup. It tasted thick as fireweed honey, but as he drank it flowed into locoweed wine with just a taste of mint.

"Now Coyote," the voice said, "it is time for us to make the other animals."

Coyote did not know what animals were, but he laughed. Perhaps it was the wine that did it. At any rate, laughing, leaning over to put the cup back, he saw into the pool.

It opened up into the hallways of a catfish eye. At the far end he saw a creature with a face covered with locust thorns and sand-burr stickers. Its body was the sagging body of a big-bellied, pregnant old woman whose hips writhed in the slow twist of a snake's dance. Her fingers, baring the long claws of the hunting cat, slipped up the hallway towards him.

"Come, Coyote, kiss me," a voice whispered. "Kiss me and you shall have all your dreams."

But all Coyote could see were the long, black locust thorns and the sharp, green stickers. And he wanted to rip out this voice that called him to the source, this voice that fired his blood chanting incantations over the dream of water. Frightened, he turned toward the door, but the door was gone.

Quickly, he drank again, swallowing the locoweed wine until he fell deep, deep into the first mists, through them into the waters, and through the waters until his lips touched the cool muck itself.

He kissed, and slowly awakened. She stood over him, a beautiful young woman shimmering in a white robe. Coyote rubbed his eyes. For a moment, she seemed to have the spined face of a catfish, but when he next looked, she had shimmered into the woman that he had dreamed.

"I am Coyote-Woman, your spirit-bride," she said. "I have come to make you happy."

Coyote laughed. The robe curled around her like twilight around the evening. He reached up and slipped it off her gleaming body.

He laughed again, delighted with her shy nakedness. He lay the robe on the ground and pointed at it.

"Lie down," he said. "Let's make love."

Immediately after they made love two buffalo emerged from the cave in the limestone boulder above them.

Now Coyote was a very potent young man, and Coyote-Woman was very sensual and beautiful. They made love a great many times, and each time they made love she glowed a little brighter. And each time, immediately afterwards, two more buffalo emerged from the cave above them.

The huge number of buffalo which once roamed the prairies and forests shows how great Coyote's medicine was, but even Coyote must sometime tire out. Finally both of them slept and that is how night came to be.

When they woke up, Coyote-Woman served them both fireweed honey and locoweed wine. Then Coyote grabbed her like a dog, but she said, "I'm tired of that way of fucking, can't you think of something else?"

So Coyote thought of doing it like two wasps. That day all day they did it like wasps.

The next morning the same thing happened. That day Coyote thought about doing it like two rattlesnakes.

Each morning Coyote-Woman pretended to be bored with the way they had done it the day before, and each day Coyote thought up a new way. They fucked in all forms of life, and each time they did it two more of whatever way they were doing it emerged from the formlessness at the limestone cave entrance above. That is how the animals of the world came to be created. That is also why women today are always wanting to change positions. They've heard stories from Coyote-Woman and they want to feel what all of it is like.

Finally came the day that must come to every honeymoon. Coyote woke up hungover from locoweed wine. He was sick of fireweed honey, and his balls knocked together like two dry stones in a leather pouch.

Coyote-Woman woke up, stretched so that her breast arched in the cool morning, and smiled. "Well, big boy," she said. "Rise and shine."

Coyote just groaned. "Woman, all you ever think of is the flesh. Men have a spirit, too, to think about."

Coyote-Woman smiled. She understood what Coyote meant. Women have always been like that. She left him to his spirit, and he turned over and went to sleep.

She wandered down to the sea to bathe herself. After all, it is hard work for a woman to fuck for almost a month and to give birth to all the creatures that Coyote could think of to imitate. For five days she washed herself in the sea, and for five days there was no glow of brightness in the cave since they did not make love. That is why every month there are several nights of darkness with no light at all.

When she returned, Coyote grabbed her by the arm. "Woman," he said. "I thought you'd never come back." He had a giant erection and he immediately started fucking her. She glowed brighter and brighter.

The more she glowed, the more he loved her, and the more he played love games with her. Everytime she glowed brighter. That is why women who have been making good love still glow today.

But Coyote forgot. He made love to her so much that she burned like a giant meteor; far too brightly, in fact, for the earth.

"Anything that hot would scorch all creation," the Great and Monstrous Catfish said. So with one cosmic gesture he put her in the sky as the moon.

Now Coyote suddenly found himself curled up beside a limestone boulder in a little ravine by the river breaks. Above him glowed a round, ripe and full moon. Immediately, as if in a dream, he recognized the hips of Coyote-Woman.

He cried out to her, but the moon cannot answer. He cried out to her again to tell her of his love and suffering, and the joy he felt in seeing her. Coyotes still cry in much the same way to the moon today. Almost any night if you are in the right place you can hear Coyote singing his love song to the moon. It is a song filled with loneliness, love, sadness and desire.

It's the original inside-gut-rage drunk on locoweed wine blues.

Mad dog, some people call it.

Others just call it the Blues.

Look at the dog star some night. If he's not there, you'll know where he's at—making love on the dark side of the moon.

DANCE LAND

William Shipley
How Old Man Coyote
Married His Daughter

The myths of the Maidu Indians of Northern California are among the
most interesting in western North America. The story of Coyote's mar-
riage to his daughter is part of a cycle of Coyote tales which were written
down (albeit haltingly) in the Maidu language at the end of the last cen-
tury. The recorder was Roland Dixon, a Harvard professor; the story-
teller was H´anchibuyim, perhaps the last great Maidu raconteur.

After I had learned the language from the few remaining Maidu
speakers in the fifties, I worked with one of my Maidu friends to recon-
stitute Dixon's rather faulty recording.

In the present translation I have tried to respect both languages—the
Maidu and the English—a delicate and difficult task. I hope it has been a
relatively successful one.

Old Man Coyote, wondering around in the north country,
came upon a house. He married and settled down there.
He stayed there, spending his time hunting field mice.
Then he had a daughter. He lived with his wife and did
nothing but hunt field mice.

As time passed and his daughter was growing bigger, he
just went on doing ordinary things. He had a son. The
coyote daughter grew into a very fine woman.

Then Coyote thought things over. "I wonder if there
isn't some way I could manage to marry this woman," he
pondered. "What if I should be sick. Then, I'll lie down
and, after a bit, I'll seem to be dying. If I tell them that I'm

dying they'll take it as a fact."

So he went off hunting and came home at dusk. After a while, when he had been lying down, he spoke. "I was so sick I almost didn't make it back," he said. He didn't sleep much that night. At sunup he just kept lying there. "I think I'm very sick," he said.

His wife and daughter went out to gather food from time to time. "Just pick up anything you can find to eat so that you can keep your two kids alive," he told his wife. 'I'm very sick, o givlt gt tll. I wonder what I'll do. Maybe I won't get well. But all of you stay here," he said to them. "Over yonder lives a certain man who looks like me. Later, when your daughter marries him, all of you can live there. Don't think about me, don't cry a lot, just live there. When your daughter marries, take whatever her husband gives you and make a life with him. When I die that's what you must do." Coyote just lay there. "Perhaps the house may burn down sometime," he said. "After you have seen my remains, go away."

Later, when the others had gone out gathering, Coyote got some deer bones together, put them in the house and set fire to it. It looked as if it had burnt down by accident.

The others came back and saw only charred bones left in the place where he had been lying. The next morning, after they had mourned for him, they went to the place he had told them to go. They found the house and stayed there.

Coyote had disguised himself by smearing his fur with pine-pitch so that when the others got there he married that woman. His mother-in-law and brother-in-law moved in and they all lived together.

Then the brothers-in-law took to hunting field mice. And once, when Coyote was digging, the coating of pitch fell out of his armpit. His brother-in-law saw it. They came home at dusk. The next day when Coyote went hunting his son stayed home and spoke to his mother. "Oh, Mother! He does just like my father. And he looks like him. He goes about things the same way. When he's digging he stops and looks around in the same way. The stuff he smeared on has come out of his armpit. I saw it! I'm sure he's my father!"

So then the mother and daughter packed everything up and they all left in a rage. Coyote came back to find the place deserted. Bewildered, he looked all around, then he went away. "I'm really a wicked one," he said to himself. "When they are telling stories, people will say: 'Coyote married his own daughter long ago.'" He walked off along the edge of the forest.

Martin Willitts, Jr.

Coyote Dances with the Stars

Coyote liked to dance
he thought
he was the greatest dancer ever
and he wanted to dance with the stars
oh he would show them how to dance
he would he was so good
but he howled with misery
because he could not dance in the sky
he howled so loud the stars felt sad
so they came to pull him up
and they told him not to let go
and they danced oh how they danced
Coyote danced so good even the stars
thought he was a good dancer
Coyote became proud and let go
and fell to the ground but
another Coyote saw the dancing
and he wanted to dance and he howled
and the stars took him and he danced
and he let go and he fell and
another Coyote wanted to dance
and he howled and everytime you see
something fall out of the sky
it is another dancing Coyote.

Dell Hymes
5-Fold Fanfare for Coyote

unwearied, unweathered, unwashed, unwished, unworshiped—
wily wencher, wiver, widower, waif—
whimsical, whiffler, whistler, wheedling whangam—
wayfarer, wangler, welsher, wastrel, wallower—
walking, watching, warning, warding, warranting—

mousing, mating, mischieving, metamorphosing!
malingering, mimicking, miscible mirror!
Misogynist—Mongrel—Munchausen—Minister—Muse!

fooling friends, foiling foes, featly transforming fiends &
finagling, fingering, fucking, forsaking females &
fixing flora & fauna in future functions &
fabricating facilely, foraging fortunately, famously
Fecund Factotum—
      Fornicating Physician—
         FOUNDER!

befuddled, besmirched, beleaguered, belittled begetter—
profane, prophylactic, prolix, procrustean precursor—

WANDERER
MISCREANT
FORNICATOR
BUNGLER
PRONOUNCER—

IT'ÁLAPAP'AS!
TÉNIQ'ÍYA! STANK'IYA!
ISK'ÚLYA!
ÉSHIN! ASHNÍ!
SPILYÁI!

never will he go from this land,
here always, as long as the land is,
that is how Coyote is in this land
(Coyote, surviving all names);
now I know only that far. . . . .

The people coming are near now. . . . .
Story! Story!

In the sunshine, in the sunshine,
All kinds of butterflies flying around!
No flies!

Don Ogden
Land Mass

A lot of continents
start out fat upnorth
then point south
in slimness:
North America,
South America,
Africa, Asia, even Europe
points south with Italy, Spain & Greece.
Australia would too,
if the Bass Straight
would dry up.
Well, so what
you say?

ASIA

I don't know!
It just seems odd.
More than coincidence.
With all that magnetism
moving around so much
and being as us humans
are so into shapes and symbols
and such.

SOUTH AMERICA

Perhaps the Great Spirit
while moulding clay into landmass
was thinking 'Hmm, this is a nice shape.'
and then, chuckling, said to self outloud,
"This ought to give those twoleggeds
something to ponder."
And Coyote heard
and went on
heading home
smiling.

Walking
in the great woods upnorth
Coyote listened
as the people said
"Where do we live?"
Some followed him
out to the plains
where Coyote made a circle.
Walking around and around
Coyote said to them,
"If skinny, head south.
If fat, go north."
and they did.
Coyote laughs.

E

N   S

W

Paula Denham
Coyote Boy Is Hungry

"Take the ax and the basket," said Coyote Mama. "You must now gather wood for the fire if you would eat." She was speaking to Coyote Boy who was playing nearby. Coyote Boy, who much preferred playing to gathering wood, pretended not to hear her.

Coyote Mama took the ax and the basket and set them down beside Coyote Boy. "You must gather the wood," she repeated. "You must work if you would grow up." Coyote Boy still pretended not to hear her or to see the tools. Coyote Mama went back to her weaving.

Coyote Boy played through the day. As night drew near, his belly began to complain. He went to his Mama and said, "I'm hungry, my belly is complaining. Let's eat." But Coyote Mama pretended not to hear and went on with her weaving.

Now Coyote Boy was VERY hungry. He began to fidget and whine for food. "There is no wood for the fire," said Coyote Mama, and went on with her weaving. Coyote Boy began to jump up and down angrily.

"You gather the wood," he cried. "You're the Mama; it's your duty to feed me. I'm hungry!" But Coyote Mama just kept on weaving.

Coyote Boy became furious and threw a tantrum as only

Coyote Boy could. He flung himself on the ground and kicked and screamed. He howled and hollered. He gnashed his teeth and held his breath till he turned blue. He began to throw things around. He picked up the basket and threw it off into the woods. He picked up the ax and chucked it straight at Mama and thunk! Coyote Mama fell dead.

Coyote Boy was horror-struck. He knew he was in terrible trouble. Who would feed him now?

Coyote Boy wandered about in the woods all that night. By morning he was TERRIBLE hungry. He saw Wolf Mama out gathering wood for her morning fire and ran up to her. "Oh Wolf Mama, may I come to breakfast with you?" he pleaded.

"Sorry, Coyote Boy," answered Wolf Mama, "I have my young cubs to feed, but if you take this ax and basket and gather wood for my evening fire, you may come to dinner."

"Uh, no thanks," mumbled Coyote Boy and wandered on. Again and again he approached the woods families; again and again he got the same answer. But Coyote Boy was just a little more stubborn than he was hungry; and he was sure he was a lot more clever. And he had an idea. He hitched to town. Straight to the Welfare Office.

Coyote Boy walked up to the lady at the desk. "Will you feed me?" he asked, looking as needy as he could which wasn't difficult; he was, after all, SOOO hungry.

"Certainly, we'll feed you," smiled the lady, and Coyote Boy began to dance and giggle, his mouth watering up and him patting his belly and feeling oh so clever. "Just fill out these forms and take them to the Employment Office. They'll give you an ax and a basket and . . ."

Coyote Boy was already running. He ran and howled and ran. Through the town he ran. Out into the woods he ran. He ran and howled. He ran so fast and so hard, howling all the while, that WHAM! he ran smack into a fat old oak tree in the middle of the forest. Coyote Boy jumped up and ran WHACK! into the tree again. And again and again till his stubborn head became mush and Coyote Boy slumped dead at the foot of the old oak.

When Coyote Boy woke, he was being carried. He was flying through the dark, a Spirit Coyote at each arm. "Where am I?" he asked. "Where are you taking me?"

"You are on your way to the Great Forest," answered the Spirit Coyote on his left, "and to reunion."

A gray light was growing now, they were circling, descending, and Coyote Boy saw below him a vast green and lush forest. The Spirit Coyotes brought him gently down and set him softly at the feet of Coyote Mama who sat weaving stars into a shimmering celestial blanket. Coyote Boy's mouth hung open as he tiptoed close.

"Mama?" he whispered.

"Yes, son."

"My heart rejoices to find you," Coyote Boy grinned, "and my belly, too. When do we eat?"

John Gardner
Coyote and the Dead Man

for Peter Blue Cloud

One day Coyote opened his door to step into the world and what should be lying there, right across the stoop of his door, but a dead man. Coyote scowled, then glanced back to see if his children had noticed, but they hadn't. Then he slid his eyes around to see if any of the neighbors were looking, but so far so good. He stepped over the dead man with delicate feet, then leaned back to pull the door shut, then carefully dragged the dead man into the bushes and sat down to think.

He thought—lightning fast, as was his way—about why such things had to happen in the world, why this particular dead man should be laid at *his* doorstep—and not Crow's, for instance—the smell of him ruining the morning. And then Coyote thought of a plan. He leaned down to the dead man and said, "Listen, brother. We've got to change the world. Are you up to it?"

The dead man opened his eyes to look at Coyote with deep disgust.

"Dead friend," said Coyote, "let me phrase it another way: What is it that interests such elevated spirits as yours and mine except Truth and Justice and the Dignity of Life?"

This was not really what was deepest in his heart, but he felt it would be wise to take the high line with the dead, at least in the beginning. Get one of them riled up, there was no telling what it might lead to.

The dead man closed his eyes. He was tired.

"Let me put it yet another way," said Coyote.

The dead man's eyes closed tighter.

"Listen, you," said Coyote, and leaned far over to whisper behind his paw into the dead man's ear, "I know your kind. Get up and follow me and believe you me you won't be sorry!"

The dead man groaned. He thought it would just be the same old thing. But he stirred one finger, then another, and pretty soon, not so steady, a little absentminded, he was up on his feet. "It better not be far," he said.

"Believe me," said Coyote, "it's not far!"

Coyote set off, whistling under his breath, darting back and forth on the road to have a look at things, whatever other travellers had thrown away or sadly left behind or accidentally dropped—but there was nothing, just junk— and the dead man came slowly behind him. His eyes were closed to slits, and he was too tired and bored even to pick up his feet, he just slid them, first one shoe, then the other, on the dirt. His hands, hanging down past his pockets, never moved at all. It took them so long to get fifty feet that Coyote was secretly in a fury and could hardly remember his plan, but all he did was whistle under his breath a little harder.

Coyote led the dead man to the window of a house and they looked in, and, lo and behold, there was a beautiful maiden kissing a chicken on the head. "Wow!" said Coyote, putting all his soul into it, "what a beautiful maiden! Look at that hair! Look at that soft, pretty mouth!"

The dead man's eyes were falling farther shut, and carefully, so the dead man wouldn't notice what he was doing, Coyote reached up and opened them a little. Then Coyote smiled tenderly, letting his own eyes fall closed a little, as if his heart were ravished and he were half in a dream, and he said, "Look at how sweetly she's kissing that chicken!" The dead man was fast asleep, so that when Coyote tugged at his arm he almost tipped over, but Coyote caught him and with difficulty led him around to the front of the house and, finding the door open, led him in where the maiden was. "Tell me, beautiful maiden," said Coyote, as if faint with emotion, "why are you kissing that chicken on the head? Is it really your father that's been transformed by a witch? or is it perhaps that you're so saddened by life that you're willing to take anything?"

"I don't know," said the maiden, blushing a little and becoming even prettier. "She's my pet, that's all. Is there something wrong with that?"

Then she saw the dead man and began to scream and bat the air to drive out the smell of him. No matter, thought Coyote, and helped the dead man back out through the door. It was obvious that dead people cared no more for beautiful maidens than for turnips. Getting rid of the dead man, he was beginning to see, might not be all that easy.

They went about sixty or seventy feet and found the part-time residence of a visiting chieftain who'd been all around the world and had all the good and evil spirits at his bidding. They found a ladder against the wall, left by some thieves who had tried to sneak into the place a while before but had been chased off by the dogs. (When the dogs saw the dead man they went slinking away with their tails between their legs.) Coyote and the dead man climbed the ladder, Coyote pushing the dead man from behind—it was hard, hard going—and looked in at the window. The whole room was filled with gold and jewels and priceless artifacts gathered by the spirits and by the chieftain's own hard work and sound business practices.

"Wow!" said Coyote. "Will you look at all that treasure!" With apparent greed and avarice he smiled up at the dead man, on the ladder just above him, and then instantly Coyote's smile turned to dismay, for the dead man, who was now in a deep sleep, no more interested in treasure than in a bundle of sticks, was tilting backward, far off balance, and would soon come crashing down on Coyote and both of them would go banging down the ladder onto the pavingstones. Coyote reached up and pushed the dead man's hind end and got him balanced again. Then, carefully, slowly, back down the ladder went the two of them. Coyote gnashed his teeth.

A hundred feet later they came to old Mountain Lion's house, and Coyote thought, what was there to lose?—he might as well try it! So, finding the door open, he went into old Mountain Lion's house with the dead man. As usual, sure enough, old Mountain Lion was doing the various things he believed one should do to keep fit. He would let out a bolt of lightning from the bottle where he kept them, and he would race the bolt to the far wall of his house, running so fast he could no longer be seen, and then he would throw himself against the wall just in time for the lightning bolt to hit him—*Crash!* Sometimes he would take it directly in the chest; sometimes, with an elegantly casual look, he would tip up an elbow and take it there, or he'd take one on the heel. Occasionally, showing off, he would take a small one in the eyeball, which would briefly turn the eyeball bluish-white, like a sapphire. When he'd outrun lightning bolts and allowed them to hit him for an hour or so, he would sit down, panting hard and wiping his forehead, and then he'd begin on his muscle builders. He would pick things up, set them down again, pick them up again, set them down again, and so on, starting with relatively light things, like the house, and moving to relatively heavy things, like the mountain.

"Wow!" cried Coyote when old Mountain Lion had the mountain over his head, straining every muscle and trembling with the effort of it, his eyeballs bulging, sweat pouring off him like water from a waterfall, "look at that physical power and fierce determination!"

The dead man said nothing, and when Coyote looked around he saw that the dead man had allowed himself to sink back onto Mountain Lion's chickencoop, his arms stretched wide, head fallen limply to one side, mouth open, eyes shut. Grimly, whistling under his breath harder than ever, Coyote urged the dead man on down the road. "Come on, come on!" he nagged.

"—be much farther," mumbled the dead man.

They came to where the people were all taking part in a great festival—Coyote couldn't remember which one; traveling with the dead man he'd lost all track of time—but whatever the name of the festival might be, they were all eating roasted chicken, and Coyote realized that he was hungry. He stood in line with his straw dish, and the dead man came along behind with his, and after they'd been served pieces of chicken and cups of red-willow tea, Coyote and the dead man went over to where it was shady and found a place to sit. Coyote ate his chicken. It tasted just wonderful, and he was thinking of sneaking through the line again when he glanced over at the dead man and saw, not to his surprise, that the dead man hadn't taken one single bite but was sitting with his feet crossed, leaning against the tree and looking dead again, with his eyes closed to slits. "Here, I'll trade you," Coyote said, and gave the dead man his empty dish and took the dead man's full one.

As he ate he racked his brains for something in the world

that might interest a dead man, and the more he turned the question over the more he realized how vexatious it was. Beautiful maidens were no better than turnips to a dead man, and vast treasures were worth no more than a 'bundle of sticks.' Power and quickness were so tiresome to a dead man they could put him to sleep even on the sharp roof of a chickencoop, and not even the rich smell of roasted chicken could entirely bring a dead man to his senses. Coyote had stumbled, he saw, onto a hard, hard question.

He was thinking with such concentration he didn't notice at first that, a little to the left of the tree where the dead man was, an old woman in black, with grayish black hair, had come with some children to sit down on the grass and eat, and the old woman, to keep the children from picking on each other or stealing each other's food, was telling them all a story. It was one of those stupid, complicated stories about Coyote and Crow, the kind of story Coyote hated, a story with no lesson or purpose in the world, not even so much as a sneaky half-virtue to justify its existence—one of those stories that do nothing but pass the time.

Coyote banefully slid his eyes at the children and the old woman, but none of them noticed. "Well!" said the old woman, smiling and rolling her black, flashing eyes around from child to child, "Crow thought long and hard about which of the baskets to open—the basket made of grass, the basket made of sticks, or the basket made of braided hair."

Coyote shook his head and stretched the corners of his mouth down. There had never been any such baskets, it was all lies and foolishness. He wished the old woman would go away and let him think about his problem. But the old woman chattered on, her cracking, dry voice distracting him. She said, "Then Crow got to thinking how Coyote was the trickiest spirit that ever got trapped in a skin, but Chicken, on the other hand, who'd given Coyote the baskets, was so witless and blissful (or small-mindedly spiteful, if *that* mood was on her) it was hard to be sure she had any spirit at all under her skin." The old woman chuckled.

Coyote stood up and, narrowing his eyes, lowering his head so that he looked like a hunchback, carried the dirty straw dishes and cups to the trash-ravine. Then he returned to get the dead man and continue on their search. The dead man sat with his eyes a little open and one large, lead-gray ear tipped slightly in the direction of the old woman.

"'Stranger and stranger,' thought Crow," the old woman was saying, "and he look long and hard at the three trap doors one with a ring-handle of stone, one with a ring-handle of buffalo horn, one with a ring-handle of turquoise framed in silver."

"Come on," said Coyote to the dead man, and tapped him on the shoulder.

Slowly, the dead man raised one finger to his mouth, signalling Coyote to silence.

Coyote stared in horror from the dead man to the old woman, who was croaking on and on, her black eyes aglitter, her hands absentmindedly picking small wildflowers mixed in with the grass around her and dropping them onto the pile of trash she already had—bits of bright cloth, gleaming metal trinkets, gray and white stones, one robin's egg long-since-hatched.

On his delicate feet, rolling his eyes toward heaven in disgust—remembering now that this had been his plan from the beginning (the old woman was obviously Crow in a typically stupid disguise)—Coyote sidled off and, when he was sure he was rid of the dead man for good, turned around, grinning, and flew like lightning straight home to his house, ran in and slammed the door and leaned his back on it.

Tim McNulty
Coyote at the Movies

We've all seen it before—Weyerhauser, Georgia Pacific,
Simson Timber, Crown—the same forestry promo film,
rundown of the industry from forest tree to suburb box;
but when Coyote got hold of the lost film can, and took a
look at the end of the reel, *he* knew immediately how to
run it, and invited all his friends.

So—the finished tract houses and tormented lawns and
shrubs, that so upset and displaced all the animals there,
became the beginning.

"Here we are," said Coyote, and all agreed.

But suddenly there appeared a whole crew of human
workers who carefully and quickly began taking the
houses down—shingle by board by window by door, and
loading the pieces into large flat trucks. In a flash the
trucks had delivered the lumber to a great lodge Coyote
told them was the lodge of Many Healing Wheels, told
them he'd been there himself at night and seen it all. Inside
the great wheels with teeth sharper than Beaver's spin all
the boards back into logs again. No one had ever seen any-
thing like this. (Even Coyote was taken aback at the sight.)
And in awe they watched the logs be carried by huge ma-
chines larger than elephants and loaded onto long trucks
which—driving backward so the trees could steer them to

exactly where they wanted to be—carried them through many small towns far into the mountains on special roads built just for them. It was such a wonderful sight even the Old Man himself had to smile. All those old trees going back home.

Once there, there were huge towers as high as a Douglas fir, which carefully lowered the logs down to just their precise spots on the hillside. The squirrels were beside themselves! But who are these blue-shirted workmen who wait in the brush? Coyote says they are shamen who possess magic wands of smoke. And if everyone watched closely, they would see them placing all the limbs and branches back onto the broken trees. Amazing! They were even joining and healing the cut trunks back together! Everyone agreed these must be powerful priests (and marveled at the special herbs they kept in small tins in their pockets, and kept adding to endlessly from behind their lips).

"They all work for me," Coyote said. But no one was listening, instead they were watching the shamen wave their wands over the stumps and the trees would leap into the air amid great clouds of needles and dust and noise— Everyone ducked, and when they looked again the trees sat majestically back on their stumps unscratched!

Now there were such great cheers from the crowd that Rabbit had to place his forepaws into his ears, and Mole hurriedly dug his way underground. Coyote, he decided right then and there that was just the way he was gonna work things. And that he was going to start that very next day, "Even if it takes a while," he thought out loud. "Yeah, even if it takes a good long time . . ."

Mahlon Hubenthal
from The Adventures of Don Coyote

coyote found a shady spot
stretched out
               dreamed of the time
               before people
of the days when he didnt know anything
and thought everything he could see
was part of his body
coyote did not know how to sleep
coyote looked around
saw all the things he was
grass meadow creek wind
mountain forests of stars
arc of sun and moon

              ●

coyote went walking one day
to find out where his body
ended
             he climbed
a high plateau to marvel
at the expanse of his great body
when a monstrous wind arose

a giant suction dragging him down
into a gaping canyon

•

coyote wrestling with the laws
of reality slid down a deep canyon
into the abyss
                bordered with bushes
and tall ivory columns   the wind
died down coyote heard voices
and the sound of someone talking
in his head

•

Ha! coyote I have swallowed you
and your fantastic images
with the truth   inside my belly
you will see stars and the end
of the universe

•

coyote summoned his tapeworm advisors
the first one said
                until we are warm
                pound sand coyote
coyote kicked around tripped
on a pile of smashed lumber
cussed flipped his bic threw
everything he could lift on
the blaze

•

the voice in his head stopped
urging coyote to piss on the fire

a scream rose in a wailing pitch
and the second tapeworm spoke
                you are adrift in space
                swallowed by space get
                to the heart of it

                        •

now coyote could see overhead
a giant heart of coal pumping diesel and smoke
through plastic tubes the size of rivers
he built the bonfire bigger
pierced the oil tube close
to the heart and the fire
exploded like a lost oil
refinery as the third
tapeworm spoke
                tell your brothers to make
                for the exits you may have
                to fuck your way out

                        •

now it was clear
he was with all
his animal kin
inside an evil
factory everywhere
the creatures coughed
and fled
                beaver
so the story goes was
the last one out
another story goes it
was muskrat   Ha! the
asshole of the monster

clamping tight on the tail
of the rat in the throes
of death
                    coyote
laughing to himself
his thing a ma jig
smoking between his legs
                    got enough firepower
                    in this baby to rip
                    a new ass

                         •

coyote carved the monsters
smoking carcass   and the creatures
had a feast   they ate away
and came to acquire their own nature
from the food they were eating

oh those who ate the dripping grease
from the ribs worked in auto garages
manned the grills in rib joints
those who tasted entrails shouldered
the urban garbage cans & according
to freud ran the banks

tasting the wing meant a stint
in the airforce eating underarms
meant an advertising career dining
below the belt guaranteed a trip
to hollywood las vegas & houston
texas which is where coyote
        was settling into a warm
pair of legs when candy came off
shift
                         •

Rob Moore
Photos of Eve

a trickster put two
pictures in my copy of
Finnegan's Wake, unread but carried
for years, that called from the bookcase
today, open me.
a picture of a woman
brushing her sand blonde hair long
before an oval mirror with lyre arms
on a wooden dresser. I stare at
the mirror and almost see her,
something stirs in my belly. she is
dressed in a dark skirt the edge of
the picture cuts off at the hips and her
back is bare but for hair. her arm
with the brush that can be seen as a blur
crosses over her breasts in the mirror,
left arm in an L, elbow towards the camera.
I concentrate on her face, those wide
loose lips, level gaze, rose brocade on
the wall behind her above what must be the bed.
morning light streams in and casts smooth tube
shadows on the curved surfaces of dresser, frame,
a scattering of scent bottles and winejug of flowers,

orange, yellow marigolds. I try to remember
this in my body, how she came to be in my book. I
turn the photo over and gasp to read
       I wrote on the other one
       I love you anyway . . .
                                        Eve
of course, Eve! and the photo side
echoes more memories: Eve in the sunlight,
looking into her eyes, lying beside me.
but who took this picture?
I pause. how did I ever know you,
Eve, how did I ever leave?
I search the picture for clues, read
both sides again. I remember the beginning
of Finnegan
                    riverrun, past Eve
and slap the hard bone of my forehead,
of course, but I've lost the page!
I dash to pick up the book from where
I threw it on the floor by the fire and
try to let it fall open to the natural
place this picture has rested while
I moved from country to country, state
to state, and obliging as a magician
making something of things not there,
it does, another photo waits, its back
towards me, writing.   holding
a finger on the page I pluck it out, read
       Phil
            I don't have anything funny to say.
       I love you and I think I always will . . .
and again she signed her name, Eve.
I turn the picture over.   a smiling
woman in a print shift is looking at me

from a copse of ripe cherries, her expression
gentle, amused.
Phil is not my name.
I compare the photos, the clothed
Eve in cherries is the only one I knew,
the other the one I recognize.
I put the picture of Eve at the mirror
on my dresser, to bring back memories.
the other I return to Finnegan for Phil,
who I haven't seen in years.
some other time I'll read the page she put it,
for now I want her brushing her hair in the mirror
I still have from the house we lived in then,
when Eve whispered these promises in my ear.
I love you anyway.
coyotes have yapped, yiked, laughed all day.

Steve Nemirow
Pissinonem

I was sitting at the kitchen table reading children's books about birds, with the door open on a summer morning, when I heard footsteps in the gravel and looked out to see my old neighbor Coyote come strolling towards the shack.

"Hey my fran!" he shouted up from below, waving real friendly when he saw me. My shack is sort of perched here on the side of the hill and has splintery old stairs leading to the front porch. I could tell Coyote was in one of his moods when he bounded up two steps at a time, rattling the place on its foundations. He greeted me too energetically, asking me how I was feeling, shaking my hand like we hadn't seen each other in years.

"And how's poetry-biz?" he asked, poking me in the ribs as he came in the door.

Now this happened one of those years when we were both trying to put a dent in the world of poetry, so I just said, "Did you know there's a hundred billion birds alive on earth right now?" Which I'd just read in one of the kids' books.

"Hey, I didn't know that!" Coyote said, acting like he was intrigued. He sat down at the table. "But makes sense, all them billion birds, when they got fifty thousand poets in these United States alone."

"Fifty thousand poets?" I was shocked. "Who counted?"

"Oh, got a list, my fran. Some guys call themselves Poets and Writers Incorporated," said Coyote, tapping his breast pocket, which made the crinkly sound of papers folded up inside.

I knew a little about Poets and Writers. They'd sent me some brochures offering to list my name alphabetically on a computer. Also my address and published works and phone number, all for only eight bucks a year. The day after they arrived I used those brochures to kindle the breakfast fire in the cookstove.

"Yeah fifty thousand poets is way too many," mused Coyote, looking around the kitchen, which was also the bedroom, for something to eat. "But your name wasn't on that list anywhere, my fran." He helped himself to coffee from the thermos on the table, turned his grin on me, and asked with a narrow eye, "Whassamatter whiteboy, your career fading?"

"Your name was on it of course," I said quickly, dodging the issue.

"Hey, of course," he said, shaking his head as if any list of poets would by its very nature include him. "But I didn't expect no fifty thousand others," he admitted. "Anyways, they listed just about everybody who said they was a poet."

"And sent 'em eight bucks," I added.

"Yeah, well," said Coyote, clearly irritated at being reminded. He said, "Anyways, it's just a fad," and took a sip of coffee.

"At eight dollars a name, Coyote, somebody raked in $400,000 off all those so-called poets."

"Yeah, I been thinkin' I better take up something less

popular til the fad dies down. By the way, what can you tell me about that short-story biz?"

"It's great. With your talent, you could make as much money as most philosophers."

At this he slammed his coffee mug on the table, stalked out the door and down the steps like he was angry, making the whole place shake again. But I suspected I knew better, and sure enough when I craned my head around the door I saw him heading towards the outhouse at a trot.

I turned back to my book. It was telling how birds swim through the air. It said on the upstroke a bird's wings curve so they're smaller against the air, so the air can flow over them easily; that the primary feathers are like fingers that separate and twist, so air can flow between them and the wing will be easier to lift. The book told it in a way a child could understand. It was like holding my hand out the window when I was in a car going fast down the highway, and it was like swimming breaststroke. I was being told how to take off (a bird jumps into the air and pulls its wings down and back), when I heard Coyote's footsteps coming back from visiting the john.

"Hey my fran, you know there's a rattlesnake hanging around your shitter?" he called again from the bottom of the stairs.

I called down that I didn't know that.

"Yeah," he said, breathing sort of hard and pointing with his snout. "Well there is, and its got some size on it, too." He leaned back against the rickety stair rail. "Good thing no kids livin' here."

"What?" I asked, by this time standing at the head of the stairs trying not to catch splinters in my socks.

"Oh, you got kids livin' with you, rattlesnake he shows up, I don't know, somebody always gonna try to kill him.

Chopping his head off with a shovel or shootin' him. Gotta proteck them kids." He shrugged. "You got a long stick around here somewhere?"

I told him there was a rake under the porch.

"Hokay," said Coyote, "you come down I show you a little way with rattlers."

"You gonna kill it?" I asked. But Coyote he was already gone. I put my boots on quick and followed.

When I arrived at the scene, Coyote was talking to the rattlesnake.

"Hey rattler, you don't talk American, but I want to be sure you're going to understand what I say."

The rattlesnake, about five feet long and two inches thick in the middle, was loosely coiled on a stretch of the outhouse path where the red dirt was baked hard. The snake was spitting its tongue out and sucking it back in, but besides that it lay stock still, with only its head held up. I could see its eyes, and they glared at Coyote, who was standing pretty close to it, talking. It was sure a nasty glare that snake had. It was what you'd call venomous.

Then the rattler started to shake its tail, which became a blur, making a sound more like a hiss than a rattle.

"See!" said Coyote over his shoulder, proudly. "See how I got his attention?" Then he turned back and talked some more to the snake: "Hey my fran, you can't hang around here. This is two-legged territory, and you gotta leave and never come back. And I ain't gonna take your word for it, either. I'm gonna make you hate bein' here. I'm gonna make it so you never want to come back again."

Coyote got down to his knees and pried loose a few clods out of the cracked soil, working them until he had a couple of handfuls of dust.

Hey-ey (he sang)
You're gonna wish you never come aroun–d
Next time you're gonna keep where you belon–g
When you go crawlin' long upon the groun–d . . .

Coyote sang to the snake in a sing-song as harsh as some-
one running their fingernails down a chalkboard. Now the
snake drew itself up until almost half its length was sway-
ing back and forth, and the hissing got louder. Coyote
threw both fistfuls of dirt at the snake, looking kind of girl-
ish with his left; but he was right on target.

The snake weaved back and forth like it was looking for
something to strike, or ways to get out. But it was dead in
the middle of a fuel break I'd cleared for fire protection, and
there was nowhere for it to go.

Coyote took up his singing again, this time with no
words, just ya-Ha-ya-Ha-ya-Ha-ya like a police siren.
Then, the next thing I knew, he pulled his cock out of his
pants and with no further ceremony began to urinate on
the poor rattler. He was only about six feet away from it,
and he had good pressure. It was your classic golden arch,
like a McDonald's sign, glinting yellow in the morning sun.

Coyote leaned back and got into it. That rattlesnake had
to just sit there and wait for it to end, but you could say he
got into it, too.

"That's what you can call getting pissed," Coyote said to
the snake as he buttoned up his pants. "Now I'm gonna
escort you on your way."

By now the snake had stopped rattling. I guess it was too
angry and confused to do anything, all covered with piss
and dust and mud. When Coyote nudged it with the gar-
den rake, it curled onboard almost as if it understood this
was its ticket out. Coyote walked the snake on the rake
several hundred yards into the woods, across the small

blind creek down there behind the shack, and let the snake down carefully on the ground.

"You watch close?" Coyote asked when we got back to the shack. "Remember never throw rocks at 'em, they got real thin ribs, break pretty easy. Pissin' on 'em gets 'em mad enough. Maybe they don't want to come back too soon."

It pays to temper any compliments you ever pay to a Coyote, on account of they're very prone to become swell-headed, but I told him I thought it was a pretty good show he'd just put on.

"Mmmmmm," said Coyote, frowning with his arms crossed, deep in thought.

I told him that there might be fifty thousand people in this country who call themselves poets, but that there was nowhere near that many who could do what he'd just done with a rattlesnake. Coyote's eyes lit up with a sly glow of speculation.

"Hey you think I can make a Coyote story outta that?" He jerked his snout sideways and back, the way he always indicates something that's just happened. Then he grabbed a pencil from the can on the table and took a piece of paper from his pocket and began to scribble furiously.

"Coyote," I interrupted his concentration. "Just tell me one thing. Does that pissing on them really keep snakes away for good?"

He looked up at me with the innocent eyes of a pup and said, "Hey, how am I supposed to know? I just now thought it up, special for you." He nibbled thoughtfully at the pencil eraser. "But if it does turn out pissin' on 'em keeps away them rattlers, hey next time let's try it on about ten thousand of them extra poets."

Charles Guilford
How I Became a Coyote

I was not always
A coyote like this. I was once
A little boy with a mother and a father
Just like you, but I got hungry
For another kind of food
So I went away, away from
The home of my father.
I went alone.

Then I came to a little river
Where I bathed. The water
Was clear there and cold
So I drank a little. A dark
Eyed virgin was bathing herself
At a curl in the rapids,
A beautiful one.
She offered herself
To me. This was in
The mountains.

After that, I became
A warrior without a gun.
In the summer I ate mostly

Roots and bugs. In the winter
I ate other things,
Things I do not like to think of
As food, and always
I was cold.

One winter when I was out hunting
Around on the prairie, I saw
His shadow. He'd been watching
Me all along from behind some stones.
Now he came out, and he laughed
And sniffed me over. I'm coyote,
He said. You pretend to be
A hunter, but you have no gun.
I can kill you if I want to.
And he did.

It wasn't bad.
At least when I got up and looked around
I wasn't hungry
Anymore. Then coyote said,
Now you are dead like me. Now you
Are a coyote too. You will
Never be hungry again
And you'll never get fat.
This all happened
Just like that.

Chip Rawlins
Visions

The old man, pitiless
cast you adrift in these rocks,
young and blind in the rough glare
of sand and dry stones,
no food, no water, no refuge
but a long unbending horizon.

Three days and you could not speak;
wind rattled around your bones
in the chill as the moon rose
and sent all solid forms fleeing
like frightened smoke.

The breastfeathers of a black eagle
touched your burnt face, soft as tears
that would not come
as the night's father wrapped you in his wings.

A silver, lone coyote
stalked you from the inside out,
a laughing star on the wander, singing
through the split mountain of your heart.

A bearded, pale elk
came to you in silence, speaking silence
from the sweep of his ascending horns
sprung like lightning from a brow
of granite cloud.

The power was spinning in your belly, dark
and sweet and vast, burning
where your thighs join
and song is rooted.

And the sun shouted red songs,
striking the drumhead of the mesa,
and you could not remain still, your
arms tried to hug the horizon
and you sang in sound
that lived before the word.

Weak, weak, the cool earth
at your back, the grandfather returned,
his hard brown hands gripping the shoulders
of this new body.

Louis Oliver
Grandfather Coyote and the Yellow Dog

The moon was slowly rising,
    a white-gold disc,
    big as a washtub
        peeking over the prairie.
Coyote silhouetted against it
        howls.
I was just a boy and my aunt
    told me once to revere
    Wolf and Coyote—
        he is your grandfather.
We call him Yaha, but you
Must never call him that—never.
    To you he is Pochah always.

Now Pochah was not a saint,
    he told ugly funny stories
    about love and romance,
    he taught us how to fashion
        bows and arrows,
    to fletch with softened squirrel sinew.

When the moon tents the night
    with its fluorescence

Pochah knows there'll be dancing rabbits,
    so he'll use his ventriloquist's
       trick
To round up meat for the cubs
    and to pacify his mate.

We lived on the bench land of the Deepfork River Bottoms—a bewitched place, a bewitched river. In the bend of the deepest part there was a large cove of thick brownish mud. When it was wet, beware! Hokpi Fuski, the monster fish, was there. When the cove was dry and caked he was gone. I have seen this place from a distance when I was a youngster.

I said that the river and the bottoms were bewitched because my people the Creek or Muskogee Indians still practiced witchery. I don't know the exact square miles that the bottoms covered, but intruders have been lost in it. On the outer perimeter there were no whites, only Creek Indians. I cannot say how long they had lived here, but it was a settlement they called Taskegee, and I'm sure it was ancient. They built their longhouse here, and set up their stompgrounds. I was raised in this environment and knew no English until I was almost too old to go to school—to a government Indian school, of course. In those days game and fish and fowl were plentiful—we wanted for nothing.

There is still a ridge of flat sandrocks that run to the river's edge. On hot sultry days the mountain boomers used to sun themselves on the rocks. Road runners (Fusketka) ran weaving in and around prickly pears. Old Coyote haunted the ledges for packrats and mice. And Este Chupko, the tall man, tall as the trees, haunted the bottoms. Now and then he would whack a tree with his long whip that resounded eerily in the night.

There were two tablerocks somewhat apart on this ridge

that showed evidence of an old, old people. Each tablerock had a conical hole that had been ground out to a depth of about fifteen inches. They were not freaks of nature, but definitely man-made. In our time we were using the pestle and mortar made from hardwood.

Near one of these was an old Indian trail leading to the river, and on wet and misty nights an apparition, an Indian woman, was often seen standing on this tablerock.

I remember once we children were sitting off to ourselves at dusk, burning cedar to ward off mosquitoes (Okeha). Our dogs, old Kissi, Pondo and Chicony, were lying about sleeping. My uncle Hinneha smoked his pipe leisurely while my aunt discussed the fishshoot with him.

Suddenly from up the road a dog approached—a yellow dog (Efa Lami) in a slow trot, tail tucked between his legs. My aunt exclaimed: "Ko! it's a person." We moved closer to her—a chill ran up my spine. My uncle said: "Don't move, just be still."

Usually our dogs never allowed anything to come close to us, but now they seemed to be hypnotized and they merely stared. The yellow dog came right by us—walking slow. I saw its eyes—human eyes, sharp and penetrating. It disappeared into the woods. I said to my aunt with quivering lips: "Iste doma (Is it really a person)?"

Gary Holthaus

Horse

At dawn Horse came drinking
Dawn Horse came, small
As first light before Sun is up
Small as Dog
Dawn Horse came
With toes instead of hooves
Nose too heavy, legs too short.

But he sure looked like somebody
Familiar. Perhaps it was
Coyote! In disguise!
Coyote could do that—
Become anything he liked—
Could have been Coyote,
Going through the changes
Preening himself, becoming
Middle Horse,
Letting go those toes,
Growing stronger, independent,
Learning to run and to be
Tricky. Equus.

We thought they all died a while.
Maybe old Coyote died too!

At the same time!
We weren't too sure about it—
Coyote is cunning!

But he wasn't dead.
Horse wasn't dead either,
Just gone from this place
For a time.

Maybe Horse is still
Coyote in disguise,
Maybe that's why some horses
Don't get tame even now—
Just stay wild and flame-eyed
And pecky. Ride 'em a ways
All smooth and feeling peaceful
Then BANG
The world unfolds
Before you, everything opening
Wide for an instant,
Sky, ground, horse,
All mixed up!

Then you know
That's old Coyote
Still hanging around
From a million years ago
Roaming those big savannahs
Raising hell
Showing who's trickiest
The toughest—
Free or dead the only choice
For Dawn Horse
Old Coyote

Norman H. Russell
Many Stories

that one knows many stories
he may speak of any ancestor
any battle any hunt
as long as there are ears listening
as long as there are eyes watching
truly he will speak a whole night
and another and another
in his mind are as many stories
as there are trees in the forest

i have listened to him
days and nights past counting
i know all his stories now
every word that was in his mind
and when he has gone
beyond any mountain not to return
i shall sit in the night circle
speaking all the stories
a whole night and another and another.

Norman H. Russell
The Children of the Beaver

if the water is not high enough
in the winter the ice will be so low
the wolf can walk across
dig holes in the house of sticks
eat the children of the beaver

so during the days and nights
while the yellow leaves fall
the beaver cuts and drags more trees
and mud to build his dam high
to save his children's lives

i make more strong arrows
my wife sews more skins.

Carol Lee Sanchez
from Through the Microscope

Grandfather's comin back
one of these days—
            he sd.
and tears sprang to my eyes
I couldn't stop
—but in the meantime
we just have to be ordinary
trapped humans and I resent that!—

third planet from the sun
movin in
Grandfather's comin back
to check us out
see if we made it
and how
and I sd:
they don't even understand
the meaning of Coyote—

all things are only symbols.

that Eagle feather represents:
did you hear what I sd?
is a connecting point

a synapse jump
to that other place we
have forgotten about.

this place is In-between
a backwards way of going home
like Coyote playing tricks again
and hiding in the Drum.

they—understand their Jung—
and long to hold their dreams awake
but cannot see relationships of:
                    bone to feather
                    breath to wind
                    sun to spirit
                    earth to mother
                    rock to sand
Coyote laughing all the time
disappearing in the desert
to consult the Badger Twins
Old Spider Woman nodding wise—
                    These reminders
                    all around us
that Grandfather's comin back one day
to tell us another dream
to call the wind
and lift the sun
and shift the morning star
while Old Coyote laughs the moon away
and maybe—if we remember those
                    long ago dreams—
                    He'll tell us
                    Why
                    we are.

Gary Gach

I.

Coyote said if I am I
because you are you, &
if you are you because I
am I, then I am not I,
& you are not you.

II.

Was it you, Coyote, first
luring me out of the drone of
my cradle, you who in my pursuit
dissolved revealing a sudden
distant lady with fire, whose
crystal earrings showed her
as only a flame in a place

of your legend?

III.

Coyote also said
if the rich
could hire other
people to die

for them, the
poor could make
a wonderful living.

Bruce Bennett

Coyote in Love

"Sure I've done it
with other women

but you're the one
I'm always touching . . ."

So Coyote
tells his women

always the same
to all his women

who always believe him.

Or so he tells me.

Bruce Bennett
Coyote in Need

"A name is breath
and breath is wind

and wind is cold
and cold needs fire,"

chattered the stranger
warming his hands.

"I'll give you a name
if it's names you're after.

You can take your pick
on a night like this."

Joy Harjo

The Returning

I don't know
who Hugo Wolf is.
I don't even know who
you are, maybe coyote who
has fooled himself
again, and me
into believing
the trickery of the heart.
What I am saying is
that it smells like almost
rain, and I am here in this office
set off from Cerrillos Road. I
study and read poems and try to put
myself in them.
But you keep coming back
scratch your fingers at the
door and that voice you always
had, arching into me.
Raw red cliffs that you
stumbled down into your own shadow
haven't kept you away, or soft
red lights and strange electrical
music that I play. I am always

in danger. A painting of Blues Man
hangs on the wall in front of me.
The sky swirls down against
a nippled earth in a drawing
that Leo sent, Che, and these words
that I keep trying to follow back
to their original patterns.
But your half-grin
is the only image that comes clear.
All the words lead to that, even
the coming rainsmell sets your voice
not mine, into motion. You can
call yourself anything you want. Maybe
you *are* Hugo Wolf going mad the way Bukowski
said it. Or maybe you are my own life
scheming desperately to climb
back in.

Jon Daunt
He Is Born

I never trusted Coyote.
I try to steer clear of him, but this time
he tricked me good.
He stole my asshole.

It was during an attack of the
farts. I couldn't do anything.
I tried to keep perfectly still,
but even that didn't work.
I couldn't stop.

So I sat down to shit and think,
and who do you suppose
came out? Coyote!
He reached up and stole the hole
that brought him into the world, and
he got away clean.

That's gratitude. It was
the only asshole I had.

Kaienwaktatsie Okwehonweronon
Ko·ko·ko·io·ti

1

"What is the word for dog in Mohawk?"
E-rar. It is the sound of a dog's bark.
"What is the root of the word?"
The sound of the bark is the root.
"What do you think of the word *dog*?"
Woof, woof!

2

Up there in the mountains just south of this great river (St. Lawrence), they call them coydogs for fear of admitting they are real coyotes. Coydogs are considered very dangerous, (one was once seen rummaging through a garbage dump, looking very mean), so it's okay to shoot them.

3

Coyotes, they say, are thriving and spreading all across the continent, even though they are being systematically exterminated.

Although I've never met a coyote or had the pleasure of their song, I feel a deep respect for them.

They remind me of another species of animal once on the
brink of extermination.

4

"Is there a word for coyote in Mohawk?"
Not that I know of, so I'll make one up:

                                        Ko-ko-ko-io-ti.

Dale Pendell
Summer Coyote Cycle

I. FOX'S SONG:

Coyotes,
Oh, I like them all right,
They have talent;
I just don't want them around
When I'm not home.

II. MANY PEOPLE WHO THINK THEMSELVES
    COYOTE ARE ACTUALLY RACCOON

Is that mine?
Oh no, I bought this years ago.
It's got my name on it.
Yeah . . . I put that on there,
    by mistake.

III.

Coyote,
    Tears follow you.
Coyote,
    Why do you leave them crying?

Coyote,
　They all follow you.
Coyote,
　Break their hearts.
　Snip, snip, snip.

IV.

Work the whole damn day,
Come home—Coyote
　Out the back.
"Oh hi darling,
　I didn't expect you home
　　so early."
Shoot that bugger
　Some day.

V.

Yeah, yeah.
　This is fun.
This is ALL RIGHT,
　Being a Coyote!
"You're not a coyote,
You're just an asshole."

Leroy V. Quintana
Wolf Howl

Jose Mentiras bet Tacha
that old vieja
he could make her howl
like a wolf
Impossible she said
so he asked her
how long it had been since a man
had made love mad love to her
ooooOOOOOUUOOO!!!

Leroy V. Quintana
Carne y Huesos

After a lifetime of sin, at forty-six,
Senaida stopped—
and started going to church
from Sunday to Sunday.

But Doña Bartola was not impressed,
said Senaida was the type
"que se comen la carne
y le dan los huesos a Dios."*

*"who eat the meat and give the bones to God"

Jim Hartz
Shambhala National Anthem

May my heart
Be empty, O Karmapa;

My wallet full.

.

Jeff Zucker
Renard and Mooch
Watch the Wash

Renard always had trouble with signs. Like he'd see a stop sign and he'd stop. Even when he was walking. Or he'd see a billboard for disposable diapers and he'd buy a dozen dozen even though he had no kids. Things like that. He could never watch a whole show on TV—he was always getting up to rip paper towels in half or to perform some other arcane test suggested by the admen.

One day Renard's TV told him to watch his washing machine. Renard didn't have a washing machine so he trucked on down to the laundromat and plopped himself in front of a big front-loader full of dirty socks. When the socks were done, he stayed on for the second feature—pillowcases.

After a while Renard noticed that someone else was also watching the washing machines. It was a local wino known as Mooch.

"Hey Mooch," says Renard, "what's on?"

"Ladies ling-er-ay, man, come over and dig it," says Mooch.

"Nah," says Renard, "I don't like to walk out in the middle of a show. I'll come over when the pillowcases are finished."

Jeff Zucker
Renard Gives
the Politicians Big Mouths

As Renard was wandering around one day he came into a neighborhood that really smelled bad. The whole place stank. It was the neighborhood where the politicians lived. In those days politicians didn't have mouths. They waved their arms a lot and farted loudly to get someone's attention.

"This is really too much," said Renard to himself. Renard then gave all the politicians mouths. But, since he'd never made mouths before, he made them too big. That's why politicians talk so much today. You may criticize Renard for this, but believe me, it was worse before.

Philip Daughtry
The Dragon Singer

Bring iz me shapin tool an me dollop
nouts changed
     ah spit ye buggors oot
       al ye buggors

it's the clamour o me Da's teeth
he sleeps on the cooch in Seghill Pit
eftor meetin wi Dragon an gettin wed

    it's mold on me noo
me bad back
an the Sight from hogs iv wierd scrumpy

   More Beer!
     (Ah'l petrify the bliddy town in a minit!)

Ah see yiz
  struttin in yer liberated jodhpurs
      smal nekkid pups
        runnin aboot wi goat's balls
      wankin on the pigheaps
    scroungin a life wi a snake's eye
warm in yer nitpecked sleep

plannin higher walls, wider moats
  fingerin yer daze
shiversharp dragonword tucked away
grateful ye divn't hae tae offer me the odd sheep

BAAAAAA! Am back.
When ah slithered oot of Jarrow Slats
    aye, ye knew this world wasnae ye
ah fed ye fire an fear
    beast giv ye
craft tae warlock wi, boon ta mek
song iv deed an stone
  for a beast ye kept awake, on the rim

aye an the wars when ye wiz dragon spit
  afore, when cars had enormous rooms
an each bairn bore a castle tae hoard the flame

AAAURAGHGH! Twas me spit ye buggors oot
me stars amang yer wisht me tongues in yer bellies
    belchin the dancefire iv dawns, ready . . .

Gies me hollow harp
  ah'l twang yiz a glint off the gem
    me gob's gettin hot
  me tail's ower lang tae pass
noo yer al sae fat wi tearin doon moontins
    aye, stuffin the land wi yer taste for iron
      an rivers turned tae steerin wheels
    an odd acre a sky burned for toast
      an not a beast tae crack yer mind a skull
not even a nip Godzilla in a matchbox destruction derby
    stuck on the telly's milkless tit

ah'l fart an Age for yer
creak an ague
    aye, ah like me meat pasty in the grimace
      ah'l lick yiz a spark or two

Am comin oot hinny!
me hungor cannae portent the cave namore
    a seen the glint amang thoo
      silver an gold mongers plannin the debacle
survival only lasts a second anyroad's end

GASP! Am burnin for a feed
    am flyin in ye
yer ribs is the Himalayan Moontins
    an yer hearts a drum wi ancient rivers
      aye, am amang you lot
am bangin on yer bones wi me empty plate

an afore ah scoff the lot
  ah'l kiss yer bonny bright eyes luv
    aye. life alone is pure bonny lass
      pure wi imprities whimper an all
  me flame is a reckonin
    am a slither-monger for the moon's eye
    open yersel an moan

aye am a local dragon
    lords an ladies of the knockin shop
      am loanin mesel oot for coffee an hot-tubs
    bring yer kids ah'l gollop them anall
    us dragonsingers are fussy
      we divn't like tae nibble

are ye settled?
  de ye have a bone for the nights?
   aright
me mithor was King an Queen iv the Sun
a real nabob
  she buggored the planet an like or bloody not
   am heor
  a flame from the cosmic gasworks
    come tae burn yer ass
  come tae mind thunder an corrupt horses

(ah'v eaten many a good horse
  an frogs iz nowt tae a famishin bloody dragon
   na more is a fat operatic cow
  tippin boss off ootside byredoor of a night
when me tiptoe wears oot an a trip ower tongue
   just aboot nigh on a smashin meat porker, aye)

ah whisper lore tae horses through thin air
  an tickle the polish underground
   wi the mention iv me flight
  it's dragon sex
 am daft aboot fire
  an me sister is Wata
   am liable tae pop up anyplace an clatter
   ah'l crap in the holy grail
  bloody druid cast that cup
 am nout but a smokin reptile on the beer

the hotblooded undergroond for elephants
  ah'v kept secret sperm count of rhinoceris
   in me knackers

for the war against IBM
(Bugger yer ma, you computerized etherized dots!)

am extinct as bad breath
            when ah spit ye buggers oot
                wipin me off
me, wi flamin throat an armor gaited soul
        a flame a yard longer than reason
                ah'l eat technology wi snot
            ah'l clog the works wi dragon spit gannor smash

aye, comin doon road wi greenarsed measure
me eyes pokin through sky curtain
        dinnae stare
            ye'll fall in
                it's deep
                aye the bloody dragondance it's lang
        lang enough tae put yer arse asleep

Bruce Berger
Toyoltita : Homage to Dobie

At night the chickens roost in the mesquite.
Out of a dream the coyote is suddenly there
As if compressed of the dark beneath their feet.
They watch and he watches, mutually aware.

The coyote grabs his tail and begins to spin
Yelping, leaping, flinging up chips of wood,
Catching them with a shake, reversing, tumbling in
Somersaults where darkness formerly stood.

The squawks of protest settle into a stare
At the fury of moonlight swirling to no cause
Until one bird, transfixed through the shivered air,
Tumbles drunkenly into a flash of jaws.

Through barbed mesquite the splinters of moonlight trace
The amber grace, the cool sweep of a tail
And feathers caught in the soft smile of a face
Like Alcibiades, beautiful in betrayal.

Lowell Jaeger
Why Dogs
Smell Each Other's Butts

When he asked, the dogs refused him.
You are unclean, they told Coyote,
you are not a dog.
So the dogs undressed for their sweatbath
and entered the sweat lodge without him.

Coyote envied the glossy fur coats
the dogs had hung outside the lodge.
He thought of stealing them,
but he decided not to.

Instead he threw the long coats
in a great pile,
and wiped his muddy feet across them.
Then he set fire to the sweat lodge roof
and said in a loud voice:
Oh what will the dogs do now,
Coyote has taken their fur!

From behind a rock, Coyote sat laughing
as the naked dogs rushed
into the cold out-of-doors,
grabbing for a coat,

afraid there might be too few
to cover everyone.

Years later, as the story goes,
with every dog zipped in someone else's fur,
dogs smell each other's butts,
looking for their own.

Meanwhile Coyote is still grinning,
off in the hills somewhere,
rolling in red dirt,
thinking how crude
to be a dog,

how much more clean,
how much more fun
to be Coyote.

Lowell Jaeger
Custer

I am more than one hundred years.
I spoke with Custer, four weeks
before he lost his hair.
Met him in a bar in Wall Drug,
South Dakota. Said he liked my boots,
asked the price of eagle feathers,
said he always did admire
hair in braids.

I said don't take this Indian thing
too lightly. I've seen them
foreclose on a buffalo Christmas Day, move
to Texas in the morning
and drive home in Oldsmobiles
next weekend, squaws
perched behind the wheel wrappped
in blankets like huge
colorful crows, ready
to run down young rabbits,
crippled squirrels.

October nights I've seen them
sing the stars to dance, the moon

floating off like a lost balloon
and drums marching mountains
into a tight circle
holding hands.

One iron cold morning, behind the Dallas Times
    Herald building,
they pooled pockets
and used me to buy more booze . . .

George
was combing his hair again,
so I shut up.
Oh they do love their fire-water, he said,
of course he was pretty drunk himself
and before I could pay my tab,
he put his hand on me,
asked if I knew any Coyote Tales,
said he'd gladly swap
for a dirty joke.

I left him
in the restroom
with his mouth full of suds.

David L. Quinn
Two Poems

Old Man
You better stay on your toes.

Out here in the country
people will still
fill your ass with lead
and get fifty bucks
for your hide
to boot.

Coyote
in the mind of man.

We've named you.

'Gogisgi' Carroll Arnett
Answering Service

You get tired of
hearing from
Coyote, right?

Well, he's long
since tired of
hearing from

you too,
you too,
pilgrim.

Live on, like
Coyote
does,

on and
on and
on.

'Gogisgi' Carroll Arnett
One Afternoon

Leaning back in
his chair against
the wall, Coyote
rolls a cigarette,
saying
      "These
two big ole
girls come round
selling cancer,
and I couldn't resist,
I bought some,
dollar's worth.
They give me a sticker
to put in my
window."
         He winks.
"It says
WE GAVE."

Ruby Hoy
Grinding Exceedingly Fine

When I was a girl Coyote looked
a great deal like my grandfather
and told me of a place
where trout gather to tell stories
of the times they got away.

My grandfather told me stories
of how Coyote got away.

My daughters are upstairs pretending
to look for dead people
so they can take the shadows from them
and turn them into angels.

It could have been Coyote who gave them
this idea, it was not my grandfather.

My friend is in jail for being
a drunken Indian,
something about an elevator,
a gumball machine, and a bottle
of sweet wine.

My sense of humor is not
what it was, my grandfather is dead,
and I haven't seen Coyote
in a long, long time.